SEVEN
NOBEL LAUREATES
on
Science and Spirituality

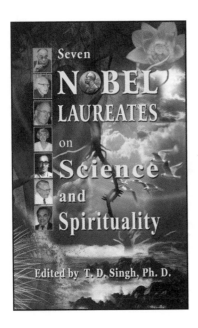

Seven NOBEL LAUREATES on Science and Spirituality

Edited by T. D. Singh, Ph. D.

Cover Description:

The cover design is inspired by the following verses of the *Bhagavadgītā* 7.4-5:

भूमिरापोऽनलो वायुः खं मनो बुद्धिरेव च ।
अहङ्कार इतीयं मे भिन्ना प्रकृतिरष्टधा ॥ ४ ॥
अपरेयमितस्त्वन्यां प्रकृतिं विद्धि मे पराम् ।
जीवभूतां महाबाहो ययेदं धार्यते जगत् ॥ ५ ॥

Translation: "Earth, water, fire, air, ether, mind, intelligence and false ego— all together these eight constitute My (Lord Krishna's or God's) separated material energies. Besides these, O mighty-armed Arjuna, there is another, superior energy of Mine, which comprises the living entities who are exploiting the resources of this material, inferior nature."

The five gross elements, earth, water, fire, air and ether (sky) are all represented in the cover by the land, water, sun, wind and sky (matter) respectively. The birds flying in the sky are representative of life (spirit). The lotus represents the beauty and intelligence manifested in nature and the clouds represent the temporary nature of material world.

Scientific research is focused primarily on the gross elements. Physicists try to explain nature in terms of matter - particles and fields. Biologists and Chemists are trying hard to combine various molecules in the laboratory with the hope that they will, one day, produce life. However, according to *Bhagavadgītā*, life is transcendental to both matter and fields and is another fundamental reality of nature. It is beyond the sense perception and its main symptom is consciousness. Matter as such is inactive. However, by the presence of spirit it gets animated, just like a live bird. The birds seen on the cover can fly because *jiva* or *atman*, the spiritual spark is within. When the spiritual particle leaves the body, the body becomes dead and inert again. According to Vedanta the Supreme Spiritual Being is the primeval source of both matter and spirit and is behind the cosmic creation. The hand of the Supreme Being or God can be inferred by the beauty and intelligence manifested in nature like the beautiful lotus flower on the cover.

Knowledge about the transcendental life is the sublime essence of spirituality. Without incorporating the conception of transcendental life in scientific fields it may not be possible to have a complete picture of reality. Thus, this cover design suggests the need to integrate science and spirituality in the search for the ultimate reality.

Cover Image: Courtesy Anderson Printing House Private Limited, Kolkata.
Cover Design: Sri Vijaya Govinda Das, Chennai.

SEVEN
NOBEL LAUREATES
on
Science and Spirituality

EDITED BY

BHAKTISVARŪPA DĀMODARA SWAMI (T. D. SINGH), Ph. D.

BHAKTIVEDANTA INSTITUTE
Kolkata

Papers and Dialogues in this volume are extracted from three books and a journal previously published by the Bhaktivedanta Institute namely — *Interviews with Nobel Laureates and Eminent Scholars* (1986), *Synthesis of Science and Religion — Critical Essays and Dialogues* (1987), *Thoughts on Synthesis of Science and Religion* (2001), and *Savijñānam — Scientific Exploration for a Spiritual Paradigm*, the Journal of the Bhaktivedanta Institute (Vol. 1, 2002). The basic copyrights are the property of the Bhaktivedanta Institute, Kolkata except for the following two papers. Permissions for reproduction of these papers have been duly obtained and we gratefully acknowledge the same here.

(i) Richard R. Ernst, "Science in the Third Millennium: Expectations between Hope and Fear". Copyright by the author.
(ii) Brian Josephson, "Science and Religion: Can the Two be Synthesized?" Delivered as part of the 1982-83 'Isthmus Foundation Lectures on Science and Religion'. Copyright, 1982, The Isthmus Institute.

Edited by
BHAKTISVARŪPA DĀMODARA SWAMI
(T. D. SINGH)

Published by
The Bhaktivedanta Institute
RC/8, Raghunathpur
Manasi Manjil Building, Fourth Floor
VIP Road, Kolkata - 700 059, India
www.binstitute.org

Printed by
Anderson Printing House Pvt. Ltd., Kolkata

ISBN: 81-901369-2-5

Dedicated

to

His Divine Grace
A. C. Bhaktivedānta Swami Śrīla Prabhupāda
(1896-1977)

A Visionary Saint for the Modern Age

&

Founder Acharya of

The Bhaktivedanta Institute

ACKNOWLEDGMENTS

We gratefully acknowledge the thoughtful contributions and the valuable insights of the seven Nobel Laureates presented in this volume. We are confident that their contributions will be a source of inspiration towards the important dialogue between Science and Spirituality. We would also like to acknowledge the editorial assistance and typesetting rendered by Dr. Sudipto Ghosh, Phalguni Banerjee, Varun Agarwal and K. Vasudeva Rao. Further, we would like to thank Sriman Vijaya Govinda Das for the cover design and Sriman Jayadeva Das for proofreading the final text. We would also like to convey our sincere thanks to the Anderson Printing House Pvt. Ltd., Kolkata for providing the background image of the cover.

The publication of this book is partly funded by the Metanexus Institute, Philadelphia, USA, under its Local Societies Initiative (LSI) program. We gratefully acknowledge the financial support and encouragement given by the Metanexus Institute to the Bhaktivedanta Institute's Science and Religion Group of Kolkata.

CONTENTS

INTRODUCTION
T. D. Singh

Science and spirituality are certainly the two most dominant forces that have shaped the course of humanity. In spite of an atmosphere of indifference and occasional rivalry, many eminent thinkers, including scientists as well as theologians, have deeply pondered over the close connection between the two disciplines. They felt the need for a synthesis between them to answer many complex problems of life. These great thinkers have been profoundly inspired by focusing on this synthesis.

Researching the life and works of several prominent scientists, such as Newton, Planck, Pasteur, Einstein, and Schrödinger, one discovers that many of them were inclined towards spirituality in comprehending their worldview of nature and reality. Their reflections are great assets to the synthesis of science and religion.

However, the close connection between science and spirituality is still not widely known among the general populace. The Bhaktivedanta Institute is bringing out this book as a part of the continuing effort to popularize the close connection between science and spirituality in the search for truth.

This book is a compilation of dialogues the editor has had with Professors Charles Townes (Nobel Laureate in Physics) and Werner Arber (Nobel Laureate in Biology), and essays by five other well-known Nobel Laureates that were earlier published under different titles by the Bhaktivedanta Institute. These contemporary thinkers explore the link between science and spirituality in several areas, some of which are outlined here:

The Role of Science and Religion in the search for the Origin of Life: We all know that the bodies of all living organisms primarily consist of 4 elements – H (10%), O (61%), C (23%) and N (3%). Similarly, only a few types of molecules like water (67%), proteins (15%), lipids (13%), nucleic acids (<1%) and carbohydrates (1%) constitute 96% of all the molecules present in the body of a living organism while minerals constitute about 4% (C. V. Powar, *Cell Biology*, Mumbai, 1997, p.7).

So, many chemists and biologists feel that life is a product of the combination of these molecules and it should be possible to create life within the laboratory. However, chemical evolutionists face a very difficult task explaining the origin of life within their scientific framework. Professor Arber says, *"The most primitive cell may require at least several hundred different specific biological micro-molecules. How such an already quite complex structure may have come together remains a mystery to me. The possibility of the existence of a creator, of God, represents to me a satisfactory solution to this problem"* (*Cosmos, Bios, Theos*, ed. Henry Margenau and Roy A. Varghese, Illinois, USA, 1992, p.142).

Professors Wald and Arber, two Nobel Laureates in Biology have explored the issue of the chemical origin of life and are of the opinion that life is possibly beyond molecules.

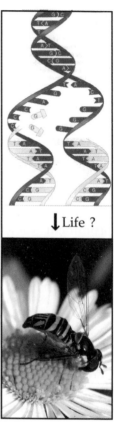

↓ Life ?

Life beyond molecules: Can we explain the activity of a bumble bee searching for nectar from molecular interactions only?

Wald proposes the Vedantic view as one of the possibilities for explaining life's origin.

The Role of Science and Religion in studying the nature of Consciousness: The nature of the human mind is very inquisitive. Even a child constantly asks, "What is this?" or "What is that?" As scientists begin to explore the fundamental components of material nature, they also begin to comprehend another fundamental property of life, called consciousness, whose presence we  all experience. Consciousness has different connotations ranging from awareness of one's perceptions to feelings, and the recognition of oneself as an agent endowed with purpose and free will. It is the very basis of all forms of knowledge including that of science and religion.

In recent times, there has been a substantial increase in the interest of many scientists in the topic of consciousness. This interest has been to a great extent catalyzed by the interpretational problems of quantum measurement. Neurobiologists have also begun to examine the mind-brain problem in an attempt to understand consciousness. Similarly, many scholars in the fields of psychology, cognitive science, philosophy, etc., are keenly investigating the nature of consciousness. Scientists like Roger Penrose are advocating the need for a new science to satisfactorily explain the phenomenon of consciousness. It could well be that spirituality will be an important component of this new science. Consciousness studies formed a part of religious wisdom long before the recent scientific endeavors took place. In the ancient literatures of India, such as the *Śrīmadbhāgavatam*, the topic of consciousness has been treated as one of the central issues. Thus, consciousness study can be a common ground for both science and religion.

11

The existing scientific views on consciousness are predominantly of two types. We have (1) the materialistic reductionistic theories where consciousness is assumed to be evolving as a result of sophisticated combinations of matter, and (2) anti-reductionistic theories, which are akin to religious views. George Wald narrates his search for consciousness and supports what Neils Bohr admitted many years ago – *"We can admittedly find nothing in physics or chemistry that has even remote bearing on consciousness. Yet all of us know that there is such a thing as consciousness, simply because we have it ourselves. Hence consciousness must be part of nature, or more generally, of reality, which means that, quite apart from the laws of physics and chemistry, as laid down in quantum theory, we must also consider laws of quite different nature."* According to His Holiness the Dalai Lama, a synthesis of science and religion is possible at a personal level as well as on the plane of consciousness.

The Role of Science and Religion in understanding the purpose behind the Universe: In scientific studies we do not directly observe most of the things we talk about,

such as atoms, electrons, etc. We only infer their existence and their properties. For example, J. J. Thompson and R. A. Millikan inferred the existence of the electron and many of its properties from experiments. But no one says, "Show me an electron or else I will not believe in it". Thus, in science the method of inference is well accepted. By this scientific method of inference we can also conclude that God or a Supreme Intelligence exists behind this wonderful and well-ordered universe. Professor Townes and Wald have discussed the specialty of the universe including life in it, which is evidence of an intelligent design. As Albert Einstein said, *"Everyone who is seriously involved in the pursuit of science becomes convinced that a spirit is manifest in the laws of the universe - a spirit vastly superior to that of man."* Professor B. D. Josephson also advocates the presence of a superior designer and theorizes that introducing the concept of intelligence will be a way to synthesize science and religion. He suggests that mathematics could be used as a tool in creating a new paradigm in which God and religion will play an important role in scientific theory. He also equates David Bohm's concept of unmanifest order with the transcendental experience.

The Role of Faith in Science and Religion: Faith is a natural quality of the human mind and is indispensable in all human endeavors. Whether riding in a bus or engaging in scientific research work, faith is essential. We dare not ride in a bus without faith  in the driver. Science and technology would not progress without faith in the experimental data generated by research. However, the role of faith in scientific research is not always apparent. For example, we are searching for fundamental laws and many of them can be represented by mathematical equations. We assume that these natural laws apply everywhere and at all times. This is an act of faith.

At a much deeper level, epistemological assumptions in science are acts of faith. Can we rely on our own observations? We have the famous argument of Descartes against empiricism – if we wear red spectacles we see everything as red. Two parallel lines appear to converge and a straight object appears bent when partly immersed in water in a transparent glass. The moon when reflected on water that has ripples appears to be quivering. Thus our observations can often be misleading.

Professor Townes presents the role of faith in science and religion as: *"...Science itself requires faith. We don't know our logic is correct. I don't know you are there. You don't know I am here. We may just be imagining all this, you see. I have a faith that the world is what it seems like, and thus I believe you are there. I can't prove it from any fundamental point of view.... Yet I have to accept a certain framework in which to operate. The idea that 'religion is faith; science is knowledge,' I think, is quite wrong. It misses the actual basis of science, which is faith. We scientists believe in the existence of the external world and the validity of our logic. We feel quite comfortable about it. Nevertheless, these are acts of faith. We can't prove them."*

Stephen Hawking recently remarked in his lecture, 'Gödel and the End of Physics' (at Texas A&M University in College Station, Texas, March 8, 2003; adapted from http://www.damtp.cam.ac.uk/strtst/dirac/hawking) that we may never have a complete theory of the universe. He says, *"May be it is not possible to formulate the theory of universe in a finite number of statements ... we and our models, are both part of the universe we are describing. Thus a physical theory, is self referencing, like in Gödel's theorem. One might therefore expect it to be either inconsistent or incomplete. The theories we have so far, are both inconsistent and incomplete."* Thus there will always be some element of faith in our scientific effort towards understanding the universe.

The Role of Science and Religion for resolving Ethical Challenges: Ethics are the finer qualities of human life from which human actions can be judged. Moral issues have always been closely connected with religious traditions. On the other hand, ethical values have never been seriously considered as a part of science. This is primarily due to the emphasis on objectivity, reductionism and materialism in science.

We are all aware that although recent advancements in science and technology have brought tremendous benefits to humanity, they have also increasingly raised ethical concerns. Ethical values have not been able to keep pace with the explosive development of science and technology. This trend is a serious threat to humanity. Thus there is an important need to generate ethical guidelines in our scientific research, especially in the fields of bioengineering and biotechnology.

Today's ethical issues have become a meeting point between science and religion. A partnership of science and religion will bring a more universal justice to the ethical issues in human actions precipitated by scientific progress. Many ethical problems have been generated in medical science involving legal, social and spiritual issues such as organ transplants, euthanasia, abortion, test tube babies, cloning, etc. Many politicians are also making far-reaching decisions on issues of moral significance such as biological and nuclear warfare, deforestation, strip mining and so on. History has shown that many of these decisions have not always been beneficial to society at large. Indeed, many concerned people will agree that in every field of human activity an ethical standard is essential for a meaningful life. Mrs. Betty Williams, Professor Richard Ernst and Professor Charles Townes describe in their articles the importance of ethics and how ethical issues act as common ground for science and religion.

Srila Prabhupada – A Visionary Saint for the Modern Age: Srila Prabhupada, the Founder Acharya of the Bhaktivedanta Institute, is the inspiration behind the efforts by the Bhaktivedanta Institute for a synthesis of science and spirituality. He made a unique contribution in the field of science and spirituality. He felt that a synthesis of science and religion would only be possible through the joint efforts and open discussions among scientists, leaders of all religious traditions and thinkers of the world.

He had many important messages for both the scientific and religious communities. For the scientific community he has left behind a strong message that life cannot originate from a combination of chemicals. He proclaimed, "Life Comes From Life" (The origin of life is Supreme Life or God) – a view quite contrary to the one presently accepted by the majority of evolutionary biologists across the world that life is a product of complex and coordinated chemical reactions. He was hopeful that in the future, scientists worldwide would in their own way examine this alternate paradigm and try to prove the existence of Supreme Life or God scientifically and philosophically. Thus he wrote in his commentary to *Śrīmadbhāgavatam*, Verse 1.5.22 - *"Human intellect is developed for advancement of learning in art, science, philosophy, physics, chemistry, psychology, economics, politics, etc. By culture of such knowledge the human society can attain perfection of life.*

This perfection of life culminates in the realization of the Supreme Being-Visnu. When advancement of knowledge is applied in the service of Lord, the whole process becomes absolute.... Therefore, all the sages and devotees of the Lord have recommended that the subject matter of art, science, philosophy, physics, chemistry, psychology and all other branches of knowledge should be wholly and solely applied in the service of the Lord.

Advanced people are eager to understand the Absolute Truth through the medium of science, and therefore a great scientist should endeavor to prove the existence of the Lord on a scientific basis. Similarly, philosophical speculations should be utilized to establish the Supreme Truth as sentient and all-powerful. Similarly, all other branches of knowledge should always be engaged in the service of the Lord. Scientific knowledge engaged in the service of the Lord and all similar activities are all factually hari-kirtana, or glorification of the Lord." Srila Prabhupada further stated, "*When the scientist, philosopher, medical man will get the opportunity to study systematically what is God, ... then only there will be paradise.*" (SPL 70-10-06) Srila Prabhupada's deep reflections on the subject matter will serve as the seeds for the development of a "new science".

We hope that the readers will be inspired by the valuable insights of these great thinkers presented in this volume. We gratefully acknowledge the contributions of these eminent scholars and pray that the scientific exploration for the synthesis of science and spirituality will benefit humanity. Lord Śrī Kṛṣṇa says in the *Bhagavadgītā* (Bg. 3.21): *yad yad ācarati śreṣṭhas tat tad evetaro janaḥ sa yat pramāṇaṁ kurute lokas tad anuvartate* — "Whatever action a great man performs, common men follow. And whatever standards he sets by exemplary acts, all the world pursues."

T. D. Singh
Director, Bhaktivedanta Institute and
President, Vedanta and Science
Educational Research Foundation

THE NEED FOR SYNTHESIS
The Dalai Lama
Nobel Laureate in Peace

As sentient beings, particularly as human beings, we have both physical and mental development. There is a big difference between these two, and yet they combine to form a human being. With the physical we have the entity, and when the human mind is combined with that, we have a human being.

Knowing this, then, we realize the need for mental development as well as for material development. Material development is needed because we have the physical. We need material things to give us comfort, and this is absolutely important. But if you ask whether material comfort alone is sufficient, the answer is "Certainly not." There is yet another thing, called the mind. It is without physical attributes — formless, colorless, etc. – but nevertheless, it is something we can feel, something very strong. Compare, for example, physical pains and pleasures with mental pains and pleasures. Mental pains and pleasures are more important than and superior to physical pains and pleasures. If someone is physically uncomfortable but mentally very happy, then his mental comfort can reduce the physical discomfort, unhappiness, or pain. On the other hand, if one is mentally unhappy, then any amount of physical comfort will not make him happy. Therefore the mental is very important.

So we need a combination of mental and material development. These two things should go together. In recent centuries science and technology have very much developed. Of course, this has been important and useful to us, but at the same time, due to this advancement, humanity is facing new terror and new anxiety. This, I believe, is not merely due to science and technology, for ultimately it is the disposition of our minds and our motivation that determine the direction in which science and technology are used. In other words, whether science and technology are used constructively or destructively ultimately depends on the human mind.

So from this point also, it is very important to ensure that inner spiritual development goes together with external or scientific development. If they start working together, I am quite sure that future generations will have better and happier societies.

> *"... ultimately it is the disposition of our minds and our motivation that determine the direction in which science and technology are used. ... So from this point also, it is very important to ensure that inner spiritual development goes together with external or scientific development."*

Science is sufficient to make material progress, but to develop the human mind, two categories or divisions of progress are needed. One deals mainly with the brain, and the other deals with the heart. We are much in need of a warm heart, compassion, kindness, forgiveness, and love. These things are very important. After all, we human beings are social animals who must live together for happiness and prosperity. No human being can feel happy in isolation. Without a friend we can neither feel happy nor survive. That is human nature. It is better, then, to live happily as brothers and sisters on the basis of compassion and love.

Every world religion has the potential to help develop warm human beings. As Buddhists, we believe that all things in nature are interrelated and interdependent. People today are very fond of specializing and becoming expert in specific fields. Of course, this is important and very necessary. Yet, because things in nature are factually interrelated, becoming experts in only one line without considering other things may not achieve for us the desired goals. Pursuing one special line may bring some good result, even unexpectedly, but it may also create some troublesome side effects. When a patient is suffering from a combination of illnesses, one specialist cannot solve all his problems. In the same way, there are problems of humanity at the individual level as well as at the group level. New developments have brought upon us so many problems: environmental problems, pollution problems, ecological problems, and so on. All these problems are interrelated.

Today, rather than this or that particular thing, we need a corrective concept that helps us to see the world as a whole. From that viewpoint also, it is very important to have spiritual and scientific development going together. After all, we must not forget that a scientist is also a human being who requires company and love. Thus, on a personal level, there is the scope and need for a synthesis. The objective is for both science and religion to work towards the same goal of supporting and helping human society. Spiritual consciousness is not at all for destruction or doing harm. The main purpose of both science and religion is to help and serve humanity. On that principle they do have a meeting point.

There is still another plane on which the concept of a synthesis is relevant. I mentioned earlier the physical, by which I meant "composed by matter." Basically there are two things: matter and mind, or consciousness. In this century, science has reached a high level. We are able to deal with matter objectively, even up to the atom. But now, with the development of ideas like quantum theory, things cannot be explained from a thoroughly objective viewpoint. And one of the things which cannot be objectively explained somehow involves all human life. Man, the knower, knows things through consciousness. Therefore, I feel that too many human resources are channelled into investigating external things. It seems a bit improper that we entirely neglect to take our studies inward. Thinking inward is not necessarily a religious practice. Even in trying to expand human knowledge, we need to think more inwardly.

So it is the relation between matter and consciousness that is important. Without proper knowledge of consciousness, we cannot fully explain external things, and to a certain extent, without thoroughly knowing about matter, it is difficult to fully know about consciousness. So there are two things. Up to now, I think, we have generally been too interested in matter, and in comparison, we have not adequately probed into the nature of consciousness. I hope and feel that in the next century more of us will investigate the self, matter, and consciousness. That will help us to develop a new conception and proper emphasis of the inner dimension, which will very naturally lead us to a genuine sense of universal responsibility. And with that motivation of a sincere sense of universal responsibility in all fields – law, science, medicine, politics, and everywhere else – we will have happiness in society.

———

THE COSMOLOGY OF LIFE AND MIND

George Wald

Nobel Laureate in Physiology and Medicine,
Harvard University, Cambridge, USA

I come toward the end of my life as a scientist facing two great problems. Both are rooted in science, and I approach both as would only a scientist. Yet I believe that both are irrevocably forever unassimilable as science. And that is hardly strange, since one involves cosmology, the other, consciousness. I will begin with the cosmology.

I. A Universe That Breeds Life

We know now that we live in a historical universe, one in which not only living organisms but stars and galaxies are born, mature, grow old and die. There is good reason to believe it to be a universe permeated with life, in which life arises, given enough time, wherever the conditions exist that make it possible.

How many such places are there? Arthur Eddington, the great British physicist, gave us the formula: one hundred billion stars make a galaxy; one hundred billion galaxies make a universe. Our own galaxy, the Milky Way, contains about one hundred billion stars. It is a vast thing. It takes light, traveling at 300,000 kilometers per second, about 100,000 years to cross the Milky Way. And yet that Milky Way is just a tiny spot in the universe we know. The smallest estimate we would consider of the fraction of stars in the Milky Way that should have a planet that could support life is one per cent. That means a billion such places in our own home galaxy; and with a billion such galaxies within reach of our telescopes, the already observed universe should contain at least a billion billion – 10^{18} – places that can support life.

And now for my main thesis. If any one of a considerable number of the physical properties of our universe were other than they are – some of those properties fundamental, others seeming trivial, even accidental – then life, that now appears to be so prevalent, would be impossible, here or anywhere.

Every atom has a nucleus composed of protons and neutrons except the smallest atom, hydrogen, which has only one proton as nucleus. About the nucleus, electrons are weaving at distances relatively greater than that which separate our sun and planets. But a proton or neutron has almost 2,000 times the mass of an electron – 1,842 times the mass when I last looked. Hence the entire mass of an atom is in its nucleus, and this maintains its position regardless of how the electrons are moving about it. That is the only reason why anything in this universe stays put, the only reason that our universe has solid structures; and that the small and large molecules that constitute living organisms maintain definite shapes and fit together as they do. If the protons and neutrons were close in mass to the electrons – whether light or heavy – they would rotate around one another. All the matter in the universe would be fluid. As it is, the position of an atom is the position of its nucleus. It holds that position in molecules, as molecules do in solid structures. The great disparity in mass between the nucleons (protons and neutrons) and the electron is one of the necessary conditions for life.

How is it that particles so altogether different as a proton and an electron have electric charges that are exactly equal numerically – that the proton is exactly as plus-charged as the electron is minus-charged? It will help to accept this as a legitimate scientific question to know that in 1959 two of our most distinguished astrophysicists, Lyttleton and Bondi, published a paper in the Proceedings of the Royal Society of London proposing that in fact the proton and electron differ in charge by the almost infinitesimal amount 2×10^{-18} e, in which e *is* the already tiny charge on a proton or an electron: so two billion billionths of e. The reason they made that proposal is that, given that nearly infinitesimal difference in charge, all the matter in the universe would be charged, and in the same sense, plus or minus. Since like charges repel one another, all the matter in the universe would repel all the other matter, and so the universe would expand, just as it is believed to do. The trouble with that idea is that yes, the universe would expand, but – short of extraordinary special dispensations – it wouldn't do anything else. For even that almost infinitesimal difference in electric charge would be enough to completely overwhelm the forces of gravity that bring matter together. Hence we should have no galaxies, no stars or planets, and – worst of all – no physicists.

No need to worry, however; for John King, at the Massachusetts Institute of Technology, has since checked this possibility and found that the charges on the proton and electron are numerically exactly equal. That is an extraordinary fact, and not made easier to understand by the present belief that though the electron is a single, apparently indivisible particle, the proton is made up of three quarks, two of them with charges of $+2/3$ e, and one with a charge of $-1/3$ e.

And now, to leave the elementary particles and go to atoms, to elements. There are 92 natural elements, but 99 percent of living matter is made of just four: hydrogen (H), carbon (C), nitrogen (N), and oxygen (O). I have long been convinced that that must be true wherever life exists in the universe, for those four elements possess wholly unique properties, exactly the properties upon which life depends.

The uniqueness of these four elements can be stated in a sentence: H, O, N, and C are the *lightest* four elements that achieve stable electronic configurations – those of the nearest inert gases – by *adding* respectively one, two, three, and four electrons. *Adding* electrons, by sharing them with other atoms, makes chemical bonds, the means of forming molecules. The *lightest* elements form the strongest bonds and hence the most stable molecules. Also, among all the elements, only O, N, and C can form double and triple bonds with one another, so saturating all their tendencies to combine further. For example, carbon dioxide (CO_2), in which the central carbon atom is bound to the two oxygens by double bonds ($O = C = O$), goes off in the air as a free molecule and dissolves in all the waters of the Earth – the places from which living organisms derive their carbon. Silicon dioxide (SiO_2), however, since silicon cannot form double bonds, ends up with four half formed bonds ready to combine further (-O-Si-O-). Lacking other partners, it combines with itself over and over, ending in forming a rock such as quartz. The reason quartz is so hard is that to break quartz one must break very many chemical bonds. And that is why silicon is good for making rocks, but to make living organisms one must turn to C, N, and O.

These four elements also provide an example of the astonishing togetherness of our universe. While H, O, N, and C make up the "organic" molecules that constitute living organisms on a planet, the nuclei of these same elements interact to generate the light of its star. Then the organisms on the planet come to depend wholly on that starlight, as they must if life is to persist. So it is that all life on the Earth runs on sunlight.

And now, to molecules. By far the most important molecule to living organisms is water. No water, no life, anywhere in the universe. I think that water is also the strangest molecule in the whole of chemistry, and its strangest property is that *ice floats*. If ice did not float I doubt that life would exist in the universe.

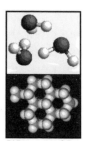

Water and Ice
Molecules

Ordinarily, upon cooling, everything contracts. So does water, down to four degrees centigrade. Then, from four degrees centigrade to zero, where it freezes, water expands, so rapidly that the ice when it forms is lighter than water and floats.

Nothing else does that. If water behaved like everything else, it would become increasingly dense as it cooled. The denser water would constantly be sinking to the bottom; and freezing would begin at the bottom instead of the top as now, and would end by freezing the water solidly. A really large mass of ice takes very long to melt even when warmed. As it is, under the relatively thin skin of ice at the surface, all forms of life, animal and plant, survive the winter, and when the weather warms, the ice quickly melts. If ice did not float, it is hard to see how any life could survive a cold spell. On any planet in the universe, if a freeze occurred even once in millions of years, that would probably be enough to block the rise of life, and to kill any life that had arisen.

Finally we have a cosmic principle. This universe is motivated by two great forces: the force of dispersion or expansion, powered by the Big Bang, and the force of aggregation, powered by gravity. If the force of expansion had dominated, all its matter would have gone on flying apart. There would be no large solid bodies, hence no *place* for life. If, on the other hand, gravity had dominated, the initial expansion produced by the Big Bang would have slowed up and come to an end, followed by a universal collapse what some astrophysicists call the Big Crunch –

perhaps in preparation for the next Big Bang. Then there would have been no *time* for life.

Andromeda Galaxy

One can suppose that these forces might have taken any values whatever. Actually, they prove to be in exact balance, so that though the universe as a whole is expanding, locally it is held together by gravitation. Our own galaxy is part of what we call our local group, which includes a sister galaxy called Andromeda, very much like our Milky Way. Such clusters, both smaller and larger, are distributed about the universe, along with vast empty areas. Each of the clusters is engaged in the universal expansion, but within each cluster gravity is dominant.

"... we find ourselves in a universe that breeds life and possesses the very particular properties ... the more deeply one penetrates, the more remarkable and subtle the fitness of this universe for life appears."

It is just this exact balance between the steady expansion of the universe as a whole and its stability locally that affords both enormous reaches of time and countless sites for the development of life.

The burden of this story is that we find ourselves in a universe that breeds life and possesses the very particular properties that make that possible. I have sampled only a few of them that I think might be most readily understood by non scientists; but some of our very best physicists are exploring this field, and the more deeply one penetrates, the more remarkable and subtle the fitness of this universe for life appears. Endless barriers lie in the way, yet each is surmounted somehow. It is as though, starting from the Big Bang, the universe pursued an *intention* to breed life, such is the subtlety with which difficulties in the way are got around, such are the singular choices in the values of key properties that could potentially have taken *any* value. Some physicists have recently introduced the term Anthropic Principle to characterize a dominant theme of such discussions. It recognizes that "We could only be present in a universe that happens to supply our needs" (R. H. Dicke, *Nature,* 192, 440, 1961); and that "what we can expect to observe must be restricted by the conditions necessary for our presence as observers (B. Carter, in *Confrontation of Cosmological Theories with Observation,* M. S. Longair, Ed., Reidel, Dordrecht, 1974).

Just to choose a few points from the already sparse argument presented above: *if* the atomic nuclei were not so much massier than the electrons weaving about them; *if* the electric charge on the proton did not exactly equal that on the electron; *if* ice did not float; *if* the forces of dispersion and aggregation in the universe were not in exact balance – then there might still be a universe, but lifeless.

From our self-centered point of view, this is the best way to make a universe. But what I want to know is how did the universe find that out? That leads me to my other great problem, that of consciousness.

II. The Problem of Consciousness

For me that problem was hardly avoidable, for I have spent most of my life in science studying mechanisms of vision. I learned my business on the eyes of frogs. The retina of a frog is very much like a human retina. Both contain two kinds of light receptors, rods for vision in dim light, cones for bright light. Both contain visual pigments based on vitamin A, that are very similar chemically and in their reactions to light. Both retinas are composed of the same three nerve layers and have parallel connections to the brain.

But I know that I *see*. Does a frog see? It reacts to light; so does a photoelectrically activated garage door. Does the frog *know* that it is reacting to light, is it self aware? Now the dilemma: there is nothing whatever that I can do as a scientist to answer that kind of question.

I have of course preconceptions. A primary fact is my own consciousness. I have all kinds of evidence that other persons are conscious; our mutual communication through speech and writing helps greatly. I think that probably all mammals are conscious; and birds – why else would they sing at dawn and sunset? With frogs I begin to worry; with fish even more. I have

"I know that I 'see'. Does a frog see? It reacts to light; so does a photoelectrically activated garage door. Does the frog know that it is reacting to light, is it self aware?... there is nothing whatever that I can do as a scientist to answer that kind of question."

worked on the eyes of many invertebrates – scallops, for example, that have eighty beautiful blue eyes in the mantles that line the borders of their shells, perhaps the most complex eyes anatomically in the animal kingdom, yet I have never seen any evidence that scallops *use* their eyes. And there is a class of marine worms found only in warm seas (Alciopids) that have great bulging eyes with everything one could hope for in any eye. The eyes yielded fine electrical responses to light, but I never could get the worms themselves to respond to light. There is no way whatever to shore up scientifically one's prejudices about animal consciousness.

One is in the same trouble with nonliving devices. Does that garage door resent having to open when the headlights of my car shine on it? I think not. Does a computer that has just beaten a human player at chess feel elated? I think not; but there is nothing one can do about those situations either.

The simple fact is that consciousness gives us no physical signals. What I have said of vision is equally true of any other sensory modality. We have no way of identifying either the presence or absence of consciousness, let alone its content.

That raises the problem of the location of consciousness. I had the joy of knowing Wilder Penfield, the great Canadian brain surgeon. In the course of his therapeutic work he had unprecedented opportunities to explore the brains of perfectly conscious unanaesthetized patients. The point is, as he told me, that once the surface of the brain is exposed, it can be touched and probed without discomfort. For some years Penfield had hoped to find a center of consciousness in the brain. I once asked him, why did he think it was in the brain, why not in the whole nervous system, the whole body. He laughed and said, "Well, I'll keep on trying." When we met about two years later he said, "I'll tell you one thing: it's not in the cerebral cortex!" Finally, in his book *The Mystery of the Mind—A Critical Study of Consciousness and the Human Brain* (Princeton University Press, 1975) he concluded:

"Because it seems to me certain that it will always be impossible to explain the mind on the basis of neuronal action within the brain, and because it seems to me that the mind develops and matures independently throughout an individual's life as though it were a continuing element, and because a computer (which the brain is) must be programmed and operated by the agency capable of independent understanding, I am forced to choose the

"... a computer (which the brain is) must be programmed and operated by the agency capable of independent understanding..."

—Wilder Penfield

proposition that our being is to be explained on the basis of two fundamental elements ... mind and brain as two semi-independent elements."

I had already for some time taken it as a foregone conclusion that the mind-consciousness could not be located. It is essentially absurd to think of locating a phenomenon that yields no physical signals, the presence or absence of which – outside of humans and their like – cannot be identified.

But further than that, mind is not only not locatable, *it has no location.* It is not a *thing* in space and time, not measurable; hence – as I said at the beginning of this paper – not assimilable as science. And yet it is not to be dismissed as an epiphenomenon: it is the foundation, the condition that makes science possible. The entire point of science is to bring ever deeper and subtler aspects of reality to recognition in our consciousness.

That recognition is itself virtually an act of creation. What would it mean to assert that something exists for which we have no "evidence"? We encounter here the deep ambiguity between being and *being known.* Our consciousness is not alone the precondition for science, but for reality: what exists is what has become manifest to our consciousness.

31

The problem of consciousness tends to embarrass biologists. Taking it to be an aspect of living things, they feel they should know about it and be able to tell physicists about it, whereas they have nothing relevant to say. But physicists live with the problem of consciousness day in and day out. The very crux of twentieth century physics is the recognition that the observer cannot be excluded from his observations; he is an intrinsic participant in them.

Let me give a simple example. All of you surely have heard that all radiation, e.g., light and all the elementary particles have simultaneously the properties of particles and of waves, though those properties are altogether different – indeed, mutually exclusive. That recognition was the basis for Niels Bohr's *principle of complementarity*, which notes that numbers of phenomena, in and out of physics, exhibit such mutually exclusive sets of properties; one just has to live with them.

Consider a physicist setting up an experiment on radiation. Enter his consciousness: he chooses beforehand which set of properties he will encounter. If he does a wave experiment, he finds wave properties; if a particle experiment, he finds particle properties. To this degree all physical observation is subjective.

III. Mind and Matter

In this talk I have propounded two riddles: one, the very peculiar character of a universe such as ours that breeds life; and two, the problem of consciousness, mind, a phenomenon that lies outside the parameters of space and time, that has no location.

A few years ago it occurred to me that these seemingly very disparate problems might be brought together. That would be with the hypothesis that mind, rather than being a very late development in the evolution of living things, restricted to organisms with the most complex nervous systems – all of which I had believed to be true – that mind instead has been there always, and that this universe is life-breeding because the pervasive

> "... *Recognizing that the physical world is entirely abstract and without "actuality" apart from its linkage to consciousness, we restore consciousness to the fundamental position..."*
>
> — Arthur Eddington

presence of mind had guided it to be so.

That thought, though elating as a game is elating, so offended my scientific possibilities as to embarrass me. It took only a few weeks, however, for me to realize that I was in excellent company. That kind of thought is not only deeply embedded in millennia old Eastern philosophies, but it has been expressed plainly by a number of great and very recent physicists. Arthur Eddington (1928) says, "The stuff of the world is mind stuff.... The mind stuff is not spread in space and time.... Recognizing that the physical world is entirely abstract and without "actuality" apart from its linkage to consciousness, we restore consciousness to the fundamental position...." (*Nature of the Physical World*, Cambridge University Press, pp. 276-277). Erwin Schrödinger also remarks, "Mind has erected the objective outside world of the natural philosopher out of its own stuff. Mind could not cope with this gigantic task otherwise than by the simplifying device of excluding itself ... withdrawing from its conceptual creation." (*Mind and Matter*, Cambridge, 1958)

I like most of all Wolfgang Pauli's formulation:

"To us ... the only acceptable point of view appears to be the one that recognizes *both* sides of reality – the quantitative and the qualitative, the physical and the psychical – as compatible with each other, and can embrace them simultaneously... It would be most satisfactory of all if *physis* and *psyche* (i.e., matter and mind) could be seen as complementary aspects of the same reality." *(Interpretation of Nature and the Psyche,* C. G. Jung and W. Pauli [each writing separately], Bollingen, N. Y., 1955, pp.208-210)

What this comes down to is that one has no more reason to deny an aspect of mind to all matter than to deny the properties of waves to all elementary particles. Pauli here is calling again upon Bohr's principle of complementarity. Mind and matter are the complementary aspects of all reality.

Let me say that it is not only easier to say these things to physicists than to my fellow biologists, but easier to say them in India than in the West. For when I speak of mind pervading the universe, of mind as a creative principle perhaps primary to matter, any Hindu will acquiesce, will think, yes, of course, he is speaking of Brahman. The Judeo-Christian-Islamic God *constructed* a universe and just once. Brahman *thinks* a universe and does so in cycles, time without end. And as the *Upanishads* tell us, each of us has a share in Brahman, the *Ātman,* the essential Self, ageless, imperishable. *Tat tvam asi* — Thou art That! That is the stuff of the universe, mind-stuff; and yes, each of us shares in it.

———

DIALOGUE ON
SCIENCE, VALUES, AND BEYOND
Berkeley, California, USA

Dr. T. D. Singh
Director, Bhaktivedanta Institute
and President, VSER Foundation,
Kolkata

Prof. Charles H. Townes
Nobel Laureate in Physics,
University of California,
Berkeley, USA

T. D. Singh (henceforth TDS): At present, many concerned people strongly feel that the moral and spiritual principles of life are being neglected in the course of scientific and technological advancement. Do you have any thoughts about the relationship between religious values and scientific values and how they can be brought together?

Charles H. Townes (henceforth CHT): Before answering the general question, I'd like to comment on a particular aspect. Some people feel that science has no morality; or that it is completely neutral on moral questions. However, science gives great importance to truth. And a devotion to truth, in spite of what one's own personal feelings and prejudices may be, takes us outside of ourselves in somewhat the same way religion can. Objectivity and recognition of our own possible errors have a value which is more absolute than our own personal feelings, interests, and dedication. That idea is very basic to science and to the success of science. One may argue that science does not take a strong moral position, but it certainly takes a strong position as to the importance of truth. I think this has great moral overtones regarding the importance of truth as well as the surmounting of one's own personal predilections.

TDS: Among scientists, physicists are generally more philosophical in their outlook of the world. For example, Einstein has been quoted often as saying, "Science without religion is lame, religion without science is blind." Do you share his opinion?

CHT: Yes, I generally agree with that. I think one reason physicists tend to be more philosophical is that physics is a very basic science. Physics is concerned with fundamentals, and it leads one to a very basic attempt to understand the universe. But there are others; for example, astronomy leads one in that direction, too.

TDS: From a scientist's viewpoint, how do you look at religion?

CHT: I think science and religion are more similar than what is generally stated. I regard them as parallel and connected. Both are attempts to understand our universe and life. So they have much the same kind of goal but are working at it with different techniques and approaches. Many people regard science as being a highly logical, step by step process, proven by experiment and hence necessarily correct, whereas religion is a more intuitive thing and not proven. In fact, some of my scientist friends have on occasion defined religion as dealing with those things which you can't prove. I don't agree with that position. I would say both are actually empirical in that they are based on human experience. They are abstracts of human experience, and our attempt is to try to fit that experience into an overall system in which we believe. One must always remember that science itself still has many uncertainties. We develop science from a logical point of view based on certain postulates. That is, we make basic postulates and from them then try to advance logically. But it has been shown mathematically that no set of postulates can be proven to be self consistent. Hence, while we seem to use our postulates and logic very successfully, the idea that everything is proven and completely certain is, I think, a mistaken one.

I don't myself separate science and religion, but regard our exploration of the universe as part of religious experience. Of course, it's not very easy to repeat an experiment under controlled conditions on most of the questions that we regard as the realm of religion. Those things which might be differentiated as being generally called religious experiences are difficult to duplicate in any controlled way because they involve humans and often special circumstances. Nevertheless, our judgement as to what is a reasonable conclusion about religious ideas is based on trying to understand human experience, both the experience of the past and of our lives. Thus religion is based on a set of empirical observations, in principle very much the way science is, even though they are not as repeatable. Also in the other ways I'd say the general structure is rather similar. Often religious ideas come intuitively; frequently scientific ideas come intuitively also. There is a quantitative difference in the amount of testing we can do which is very striking, but logically I don't think there is a basic difference.

TDS: In scientific work, inspiration, or sudden insight, plays an important role. For example, Gauss was once perplexed with some mathematical riddles. After a sudden flash of insight revealed the solution, he claimed that the answer was given to him by God, not by his own intelligence. Was this an example of an experience common to both science and religion?

CHT: Yes, I am generally sympathetic with that approach. Certainly many new ideas are intuitive. We don't know just how they arrive, but one can question whether they are specifically given by God, unless we take the not unreasonable position that everything is given by God. In any case, I see no justification in a sharp differentiation. It is difficult to trace the origin of some reasoning, so we often attribute it to inspiration, as is characteristic of many religious insights.

TDS: In other scientific fields, such as microbiology and molecular biology, well known scientists like Crick, Watson, and others favor the idea that everything is created not by God but by some arrangement of nature. What do you think about this?

CHT: Again I wouldn't differentiate between the two. However, there is a point of some importance that the question brings up. It involves the amount of development and degree of our understanding in the field of biology. If you consider physics in the nineteenth century, it is clear that most physicists of the time felt it was necessary to believe in determinism. Science in general, and certainly physics, implied a completely deterministic world. But as physics was explored more deeply, it encountered the ideas of relativity,

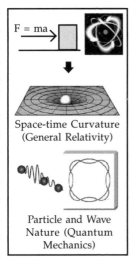

Space-time Curvature
(General Relativity)

Particle and Wave
Nature (Quantum
Mechanics)

which changed our views. Relativity was not undeterministic, but it changed our views radically from those which were held previously. Then came quantum mechanics, which clearly destroyed determinism. Some scientists keep thinking that perhaps quantum mechanics is wrong in this respect, because the lack of determinism seems so peculiar. But every new experiment done to test this question disproves the idea of determinism. It simply is not the case. So physicists, on exploring more deeply, have often found that they had to change their basic ideas. Physics of the past was not wrong in detail, but quite wrong in general outlook and philosophy. The physics of Newton was correct where it was applied, but we now recognize it as very misleading in other areas. The biologists may possibly run into a similar situation, and somehow their ideas may be changed radically when they understand living

> "... physicists, on exploring more deeply, have often found that they had to change their basic ideas. ... The biologists may possibly run into a similar situation, and somehow their ideas may be changed radically when they understand living organisms more deeply."
>
> — Charles Townes

organisms more deeply. I don't know that, but simply pose it as a reasonable possibility. Biologists are still working on a level which is simple and mechanistic in the sense that it involves primarily the action of individual atoms and molecules. It is clear that many life processes may be very difficult to understand on that basis. Whether we will ever come to the point where biologists have to change their views radically is something no one can predict with certainty. However, I would think it likely that when we really understand living organisms better, science might be different and biologists may be induced to take a somewhat different point of view.

Pawan K. Saharan (Bhaktivedanta Institute member; henceforth PKS): Don't you think that biological systems are more complex than mere physical systems?

CHT: I would say that in physics we set up certain simple situations to study. The biologists do that to some extent, too, but at least at present they can't set up a really simple organism that's living. That seems to be impractical. In physics also there are complex systems. For example, our earth as a whole is a very complex system if we try to explain all the details of all its atoms. So there are complex physical systems, but it is certainly true that biological systems are more complex than those which physicists typically deal with in the laboratory.

PKS: It seems to me that molecular biologists have a tendency to be overenthusiastic, to make very bold statements regarding life and its origin without having complete scientific proof. Today, almost all college and university textbooks of biology or molecular biology state that the laws of life are completely understood in terms of quantum mechanics and that life is simply a combination of atoms and molecules. In saying this, biologists tend to discredit the moral, spiritual, and higher purpose of life. What are your feelings about these?

CHT: Biology is a new field about which one can be very enthusiastic. It is making a great deal of progress, so it is understandable that biologists feel an enthusiasm and a conviction that they may be able to do almost everything. We must give them time and wait to see the outcome.

TDS: Religion is usually understood in terms of rituals. People think, "I belong to this or that type of religion." But the true Vedic tradition discourages the sectarian spirit and puts a strong emphasis on actually knowing the nature of the individual being, the Supreme Self, and the relationship between them. In that way, it is the science of religion. The whole idea of Congresses which we organize is to bring together scholars in the fields of sciences, philosophy, and theology and have them discuss scientific and religious principles in terms of broader concepts, including a closer look into human life and its purpose. I'm suggesting that religious rituals alone should not be regarded as the true principle of religiosity, nor should they be a barrier among people from various cultural and national traditions. Open dialogues about this should benefit all of us.

CHT: I would generally agree with that. I don't set much importance on the normal kinds of rituals. They are not unimportant, but to me have no absolute significance. I would go further and say that I don't believe our understanding of religion is complete yet, and we must be prepared to learn and change as time goes on.

PKS: In his book *Of Molecules and Man* (1966), Crick stated that the symptoms and characteristics of life could be explained merely by physical and chemical laws. What is your view on that?

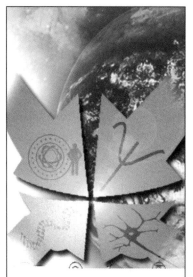

"...I look at science and religion as both working on the same problem, namely the understanding of what our universe and our life are all about. ... they will meet and join in a close knit way."

— Charles Townes

CHT: Of course, no one really knows, but I would think it is true only in a certain sense. Remember that I look at science and religion as both working on the same problem, namely the understanding of what our universe and our life are all about. I hope that each approach will be successful and that they will meet and join in a close knit way. Science may be able to explain much more than it now explains. However, I doubt we will be able to know everything, either from a religious or a scientific point of view. Certainly we ought to be able to make progress in science and understand a great deal more than we do now. But I think one must be cautious in recognizing that science, in doing that, may itself change a great deal. If you look again at physics, it is evident that in the nineteenth century physicists and scientists in general felt they were going to explain most things in a deterministic way. Many confronted the religious world with this determination and left no room for divine action. With physical laws and conditions completely set beforehand, it was just a matter of working out the equations of a deterministic world to foresee all of the future. Thus, the natural conclusion was that if science advanced, it would be able to explain everything this way. Actually, in a sense, science has now explained a lot more. But as quantum mechanics came into view and allowed us to understand much more about atoms and molecules, we found a surprising world in which science itself changes. I believe such a process is what we must expect. Science should indeed make much progress and allow us to understand much more about life, but the nature of science itself will change. So one must not think of science only in terms of our present understanding.

TDS: What is your opinion about the social and moral responsibilities of scientists towards the well being of society? Sometimes scientific products are misused, not necessarily by scientists, but by some other group, as, for example, in the use of nuclear weapons by politicians. Do you think that allowing scientists to participate in making decisions of great consequence would help to control the misuse of science?

CHT: Scientists can certainly be helpful by participating actively in decisions about the use of science and in trying to foresee the likely results of scientific discoveries. However, we must recognize that the results of scientific research are typically unpredictable. We must deal with problems as

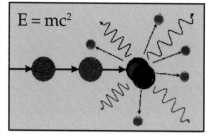

they appear, and in the human context of the time. One never knows just what good or harm a given scientific idea may produce. Consider, for example, Einstein's theory of relativity. One might say it was responsible for the atomic bomb, because it produced the idea of conversion of matter into energy. Is Einstein to be blamed for that? Could anyone have foreseen it? I don't think so. Relativity was an important idea from which we've learned a great deal and which has been applied in a variety of ways. Atomic energy itself can produce much needed energy, of course, when used in the right way. The consequences of scientific ideas are simply not predictable enough to allow careful prior decisions about its good or bad effects.

Science by and large has helped mankind's physical welfare and potentialities enormously. The increasing power that science provides can help mankind but also provide ways to injure people. I don't think one wants to stop science. If we are going to learn how to cure cancer, for example, then we're also going to know how to cause cancer. These two things are inseparable and simply present mankind with the ever more cogent problem of how to behave morally. We have had that problem since the beginning; we can injure people in a variety of ways with fingernails, rocks, or with more sophisticated tools. Science clearly doesn't change the problem, but it does increase potentialities. We need to work all the more intensely at increasing our sense of moral responsibility so that the ongoing problem of evil can be dealt with. I think it would be unproductive and would hurt mankind to stop the advance of knowledge.

TDS: We don't want to stop science, only to create policies which prevent its misuse.

CHT: I believe strongly in the participation of scientists in the political process. But we must be careful not to assume that the use of science is the scientist's problem alone. It is a human problem, not basically a scientific one. Scientific advances simply emphasize this human problem. Furthermore, we must be careful about the idea that the results of a given line of basic scientific research are predictable, or that a few knowledgeable scientists with good moral instincts can always make the appropriate policy decisions. The advancement of science as a whole and the consequent increase of mankind's potentiality poses ever more poignantly the problem of good and evil. Scientists can help society understand some of the technical aspects of problems. However, the choice between good and evil is a basic human one which must be made by society as a whole, and can only be wisely made if individuals act and society itself is based on appropriate moral principles.

PKS: Students would be highly benefited if they received training about the science of spiritual knowledge and the higher values of life. Courses on moral science and philosophy could be included in the educational curriculum. Then the masses of humanity could better understand the meaning of the proper use of scientific knowledge.

CHT: I think courses in moral philosophy are very valuable in colleges, universities, or high schools. But while courses in philosophy, moral ideas, or civilization and its meaning (including the meaning of science) would be quite valuable, I don't think one can practically combine these with, say, quantum mechanics. Moral philosophy should be taught overtly. But it is also important that teachers have a moral sense, which most of them do. A broad education must certainly deal with philosophy, religion, and ethics. Unfortunately, philosophical research is presently in a rather esoteric phase, emphasizing mathematical logic. It doesn't deal very directly with moral

> *"I don't think it is practical to keep scientific and spiritual cultures separate."*
>
> — Charles Townes

questions. Classical philosophy tends to do that more and to help students think about the meaning of life, of civilization, and of mankind's role rather than mathematical logic. The latter is important in itself, but doesn't produce the same inducement for the student to think about what he is living for.

TDS: Recently in India, the change in the concept of living has become very visible. A shift of values seems to be developing among college students, who are very enthusiastic about modern ways of living. However, many concerned leaders say that India should develop both its spiritual and scientific culture. Do you have any message for the students in India?

CHT: Well, perhaps so. They certainly should value and appreciate their religious culture, and, of course, classical Indian culture has an important bearing on the meaning of life as well as on values. But also, people who study science are often at the same time thoughtful about the meaning of life and values. I would not separate the two. To separate science and Indian culture could be harmful, producing a dichotomy of choice to go either this way or that way. Of course, classical Indian culture bears importantly on these subjects. I don't think it is practical to keep scientific and spiritual cultures separate.

TDS: Thank you, Professor Townes.

ROLE OF SCIENCE AND RELIGION FOR PEACE AND THE HUMAN FAMILY

Betty Williams

Nobel Laureate in Peace, Ireland

Historically, science and religion have lived in very different worlds. Many scientists have denied the very existence of God; others have shunned religion of any kind, possibly viewing religion in and of itself to have been the cause of the greatest loss of human life in this world we live in. And, many men and women of science have done incredible things to help and advance humankind in the field of medicine and inventions. We think of electricity, wireless telephones, technology, computers, etc., as prime examples. Other scientists, however, have concentrated on destruction, creating weapons of such magnitude that they can wipe out hundreds of thousands of people, some (the neutron bomb for instance) without putting a scratch on a building. And then, of course, there is biological warfare. What kind of madness of the mind and emptiness of the soul allows scientists to create such horrors. It is to these scientists we plead and ask the question. Why do you not believe in the divine Creator, but believe only in the universe? Why then do you not protect this wondrous universe?

Science has reached the stars and beyond, and men have walked on the moon. God willing, we will find no life on other planets for we would surely destroy it. Before science can advance any further, may God reach the hearts and souls and brains of those involved in the science of death and destruction and change their hearts and minds sufficiently, thereby allowing them to work for life and Creation. What a power for good would be unleashed! Wow! We could change the world very quickly. Everyone would benefit: men, women and children. The hungry would be fed, the sick would have access to incredible medical breakthroughs, a cure would be found for AIDS and cancer and many of the destructive bacteria and viruses that attack the human body.

These are not the writings of some idiotic idealistic fool, rather, they are the words of a woman who has seen first hand how whole societies can be changed and transformed using the techniques of non-violence. Perhaps we should be educating our scientists in those techniques.

As for the human family, the God of my understanding, a gentle and kind Father, must weep as he looks down on the children he created, for the family he loves is indeed very ill. "The Human Family", born with intelligence and self-will, seems sadly lacking in the areas the Creator wanted us to excel in compassion, love of one another, brotherhood, forgiveness and understanding.

"The Human Family." Religious leaders use it in their sermons. Politicians use it in their campaigns. Professors use it in their classrooms.

"The Human Family", how easily these words roll off the tongue. It makes me sad and yet I wonder what kind of family, in a world that is capable of feeding itself, allows her children to starve. What kind of family allows the development and use of weapons of mass destruction. What kind of family allows her elders and leaders to justify these weapons and tell her members it's "for defense". I feel sure the family members who perish as a result of this so-called defense are very grateful that they are being so well defended!

As we move forward into this new millennium, let us commit ourselves to working for a just, peaceful, and nonviolent world where the madness in our family can be treated and cured. Only then can we become a true human family.

———

T. D. Singh greeting His Holiness the Dalai Lama who graciously inaugurated the "First World Congress for the Synthesis of Science and Religion", Bombay, January 1986.

Discussion with Prof. George Wald, a Nobel Laureate in Biology, from Harvard University, USA who delivered the Keynote Address in the "First World Congress for the Synthesis of Science and Religion", Bombay, January 9-12, 1986.

With Prof. Charles H. Townes, Nobel Laureate in Physics from the University of California, Berkeley who delivered the Keynote Address of the "Second World Congress for the Synthesis of Science and Religion", Calcutta, January 9-12, 1997.

With Ms. Betty Williams, Nobel Laureate in Peace during the Golden Jubilee Celebration of the United Nations in San Francisco, 1995.

With Prof. Richard Ernst, Nobel Laureate in Chemistry in his laboratory at Zurich, Switzerland.

With Prof. Werner Arber, Nobel Laureate in Physiology and Medicine at the University of Basel, Switzerland.

SCIENCE AND RELIGION:
HOW TO MAKE THE SYNTHESIS?

B. D. Josephson

Nobel Laureate in Physics, Cavendish Research Laboratories,
Cambridge University, Cambridge, UK

1. Why the Gulf Between Science and Religion?

One of the reasons why in this series of lectures we're talking about the convergence of science and religion is that a couple of centuries ago science and religion started to diverge – each wanted to take over the whole territory of knowledge to itself, science thinking everything could be explained scientifically, and religion, possibly as a kind of reaction to what the scientists were doing, believing everything could be explained in religious terms. And so we have a situation at the present time where there is essentially zero overlap between science and religion: you don't find in a scientific paper somebody saying, for example, such and such a phenomenon was an instance of God deciding to intervene for some reason. So just from the fact that scientific work makes no mention of God, we see that science and religion are at the present time totally separated from each other. But things are beginning to change, and overlapping views are beginning to be found. However, the fact remains that science gets on quite well without God, and perhaps we should look into the reasons why this might be. I'm going to assume that most of you accept the existence of God and that therefore there actually is something to be explained: for the atheist, God doesn't exist, and this is sufficient reason why science needn't mention God. But if we assume God does exist, then why hasn't He appeared in scientific experiments? I'd like to indicate two factors which may be relevant.

First, science casts the spotlight which it uses to search for knowledge very selectively; in other words, what scientists choose to look at, to try to explain in scientific terms, is rather restricted, rather biased. And the content of science is biased in a materialistic direction. This applies to almost all the sciences, the physical sciences as well as the biological sciences. The reason is largely due to the fact that it is easier to study quantitatively the behavior of matter and the grosser aspects of behavior (both animal and human) than it is to study higher human behavior where the influence of God might be significant. So science, in choosing the simpler problems to examine first, tends always to look in directions where theological concepts are not very relevant.

Secondly, even within a particular field, science likes to look at simple phenomena, as these are more easily connected with fundamental laws. Then one tends to say, "We can explain the simple phenomena very well now; eventually we'll be able to explain the complex phenomena as well." The gap between simple and complex phenomena is one which scientists tend, just as a matter of faith, to assume (especially if they are of materialistic orientation) will be bridged without invoking any higher being. For example, the question of how man came into existence is assumed to be a problem which will be solved in the future, when we have filled in all the details (and again, it is supposed by people working in artificial intelligence that problems of higher human skills will be solved in just a matter of twenty years or so more research). But perhaps this is questionable, perhaps this gap cannot be bridged, and when we reach the complex end, we may get phenomena which can be validly explained only by saying God had a hand in them.

I've been talking so far about the materialistic

orientation of science. Now, there are two ways in which one could approach the issue of whether God has an influence on Nature. One is to continue following the traditional, materialistic line of explanation, seeing if it really does explain everything. That would be a very long job it might be a couple of centuries, perhaps, before we would get an answer that way. An alternative approach for the scientist is to say, "Let's investigate the opposite view, i.e., that perhaps we should be taking God into account in science; what would a science look like which had God in there playing a part, accounting thereby for particular phenomena?" In the rest of my talk I'm going to be making an extremely crude and rough sketch of what such a science, which we may have in the future, may look like.

> *"...what would a science look like which had God in there playing a part, accounting thereby for particular phenomena?"*

2. Intelligence as the Bridge

There are various ways into this problem, and the way I'm going to take to get in is to say that if we want to put God into science, then the primary feature of God, the one which is most closely connected with the science we've got, is God's intelligence and God as a supreme being is perhaps a little like us, but at a very much higher level of intelligence. What I want to suggest is that the new science which includes God will start by understanding and describing "being intelligent." One of the reasons for thinking this to be a good thing to do is that intelligence as a phenomenon in itself is inadequately dealt with in most branches of science, except perhaps cybernetics. Intelligence is something which in science is generally studied in terms of details, and not as a general phenomenon. There is a kind of gap here in our world view; filling it in may give an expanded world view, in which the supreme intelligence, God, may fit naturally.

Let me now put this on a more concrete basis by going over an old theological line of argument with which you are probably familiar. This is the argument that one can see that God exists through the design in nature everything in nature functions in a very precise manner, just as if someone had set it all up by writing blueprints and saying, "This is how the world should be." This is the old theological viewpoint, that one just sees, looking round one, that the only reasonable explanation for all this is that there was a designer who made things this way. Of course, this is the one which has been under attack by science for a long time, because science has attempted to show that everything that religious people had explained by invoking God could be explained in scientific terms instead; for example, the existence of man is "explained" in terms of the evolution of species.

Now, the question is: does this kind of explanation actually explain facts like the existence of man? Consider the following situation: a house is being built, and a scientist on Mars is looking through a powerful telescope at what is going on (the bricks moving about and being assembled into the structure of the house, etc.). He might well say, "I can explain all this. Peoples' muscles are contracting because of impulses coming down to them from the brain, which makes the arms move about, and as a result, the bricks get lifted. I can go through my calculations and see that the motion of every brick is exactly as given by the laws of mechanics, the laws governing the transmission of nerve impulses, and the contraction of muscles and so on." So science has explained everything; it has explained the building of the house. Everything just follows the ordinary laws of physics and we don't have to bring in the idea of intelligence at all.

But in this case we know that the explanation is incomplete, or at any rate misleading: it is the human being's intelligence and his knowledge of how to move things which is responsible for the house being built and which is a precondition for the whole process to be possible at all. Moreover, the arrangement of bricks is a consequence of the existence of a blueprint which somebody made because he knew how to design houses and so forth. It is quite possible that the current scientific explanation for the existence of man may be equally inadequate. The actual situation (paralleling the situation in the example of the man building a house) may be that every step in evolution follows the laws of science, but a number of choices are predetermined by a pre-existing intelligence. The argument would be that God's plan blended with the phenomena already studied by science and directed the process of evolution. Let me make it quite clear before I go on that no such hypothesis has actually been proved, but merely that it is a perfectly logical and consistent possibility. What would have to be done to evaluate this possibility would be to find some criterion by which one could discriminate clearly between the two kinds of explanation.

Let me emphasize the moral to be drawn from the above discussion. It is that when intelligence is present, we don't decide on its presence or absence just by seeing whether the laws of physics are obeyed; intelligence is not like a new energy source. The presence of an intelligence manifests itself via the presence of or the creation of states which are *a priori* extremely unlikely:

> "The presence of an intelligence manifests itself via the presence of or the creation of states which are a priori extremely unlikely... intelligence manifests itself by making certain unlikely situations appear."

states such as all the bricks fitting neatly to form a house, all being put together in the right way. That is, intelligence manifests itself by making certain unlikely situations appear. And this is the sort of thing that would be studied in a very general theory of intelligence. In other words, if we develop the relevant mathematics we might be able to see certain general principles at work, and we might then be able to perceive the fact that such and such happening suggests the presence of an intelligence — it would be too unlikely to have happened by chance. So, the way this approach would go through, if it were possible to carry it through, would be to say that the principles of intelligence are universal, and we can actually understand what God is about at some sort of level by just scaling up what we know about human intelligence. Intelligence itself is a universal thing, but in our theories we will have taken adequate account of the differences of degree, and of the differences in the domains of operation of the two types of centers of intelligence.

3. Using Evidence From Religion and From Direct Experience

If we wanted to follow up this approach in detail, we would have to put in some facts about the domain in which God operates. At this point we would have to turn to the theological evidence. Various sources such as the scriptures, or individuals who have evolved to an enlightened state, would provide information about how God goes about His works, whether He has other beings to help Him, and what His motivations are and so on — some of this is in the scriptures and some is not. In other words, we can start to do what theologians are already trying to do, but treat it more scientifically, perhaps even develop appropriate mathematics.

But the scientist is not keen on taking religious doctrine on authority. He likes to observe and to experiment. And here we get on to areas which are perhaps more controversial. We become involved not with religion as it is usually understood but with mysticism. Mysticism is not widely appreciated even by people who regard themselves as religious, and so in order to avoid various kinds of misconceptions I should like to make first of all a number of preliminary comments.

I see mysticism and religion as things which are intimately related and yet different from each other in important ways. I see mysticism as involving a more drastic change in the individual than is involved in ordinary religion. A mystic or someone trying to follow a path of enlightenment is trying (a bit like an athlete going through special training programs to enable him to be better physically) to follow a special training program (meditation or something similar) which enables him to have closer contact with the Absolute. And the mystic hopes to be able to see clearly into God's domain, whereas a person who doesn't go in for such intensive development may be in contact with God, but through a less direct channel. Now, what one finds if one studies the various forms of mysticism is that the doctrines of the mystics are much less diverse than are religious doctrines. My interpretation of this is that mysticism is concerned with very fundamental laws of God and His relationship to man and other worlds beside the earthly world. Whereas religion is a more applied sphere of activity, it is concerned with the question, given that certain facts are the case, how should we live our lives? So the upshot of this is that

I consider mysticism to be something universal like science, and that is the first point; and then the second point is that religions are based on the facts of this science. Thus mysticism is a kind of universal foundation for the diverse and different religions.

I should mention here that I'm not talking entirely about Eastern mysticism, because there is Western mysticism as well: e.g., Christian mysticism, Islamic mysticism (Sufism), and Jewish mysticism. These all say rather similar things.

After this rather lengthy detour, let me get back

> *"... m y s t i c a l experience by self d e v e l o p m e n t through meditation, etc., is not only the key to one's own development but also the key to understanding what is going on, the key to putting this attempt to synthesize science and religion on a solid foundation."*

and say that a corollary of this is that mystical experience by self development through meditation, etc., is not only the key to one's own development but also the key to understanding what is going on, the key to putting this attempt to synthesize science and religion on a solid foundation. And what I'd like to suggest is that if we follow this path of a synthesis of science with religion (using meditation as an observational tool), what we are doing is using our own nervous systems as instruments to observe the domains in which God works. Ordinary scientific instruments like telescopes, galvanometers, and particle detectors are not going to be good in this context because they are designed to function in the material domain. Our nervous systems, on the other hand, are designed to allow us to interact not only with the material level of existence but also with the spiritual levels, and we can interact also with such intermediate levels as the so called celestial levels (or astral planes). And so all the different levels are open to exploration if we develop our nervous systems so that they tune in. One can imagine that this would be a part of the scientific training of the future; scientists working in this field would try to develop their nervous systems so that they could explore these regions.

These explorations would be different in one interesting respect from ordinary scientific explorations. Much of the research would involve not finding new knowledge, but verifying what mystics have already said. This is because mysticism is very highly developed already: sources like the *Vedas* and the *Kabbalah* have said a great deal about the nature of the regions to be explored, and so a scientist trying to explore these regions will largely be covering known territory. However, he will be covering it from a different point of view, and perhaps trying to describe it mathematically.

4. Science and Mysticism

Now I want to cover a subject which most of you are probably familiar with, and that is the work that has been done in the area of relating science and mysticism. This explosive growth was started off by a book by Fritjof Capra, *The Tao of Physics*. Capra is a scientist working in the field of high energy physics, who has himself gone through techniques to explore mystical experience. So his book, more than many others, is based on knowledge of both realms, and in this book he describes the many connections, or corresponding similar patterns, linking modern scientific discoveries and features of mysticism. Capra's book, it should be clearly stated at this point, is in no way (as has been suggested rather often by reviewers lacking knowledge of mysticism) an exercise in which somebody looked through what scientists said, looked through what mystics said, and thought, "Ah! This quotation looks like that, so there's a connection." It certainly isn't that. Capra is very familiar with what is involved in both fields, and I believe that the connections he wrote about in his book are deep and fundamental.

Capra's connections are of a very general kind. The scientist would like to know the connections at a more detailed level. Capra, in fact, was rather pessimistic about the possibility of making a detailed connection between science and mysticism: he says that mysticism deals with the roots of reality (that is, closest to God or the Absolute), while science deals with the branches, and these are totally different things, and we shouldn't expect to be able to connect them. My own belief is that mathematics may come to our aid and allow us to connect these two things. It is one of the striking features of science that mathematics is able to join together extremely diverse phenomena. Therefore I feel that Capra is being pessimistic in saying that we will never succeed in joining science and mysticism together.

Another book which has recently appeared, written by David Bohm, embodies to some extent the initial stages of this process. Much of this book is qualitative, but Bohm and co workers are trying to work on the mathematics involved, and I think that they are making progress. Bohm doesn't talk much about mysticism explicitly in his book, but nevertheless it is very much based on mysticism. He approaches things from the direction of science. For many years (even before his involvement with mysticism) he has been concerned with an attempt to resolve some of the paradoxes thrown up by quantum mechanics, some of which I shall be describing. These present great difficulties of a philosophical nature. Most scientists just sweep these philosophical difficulties under the rug, but Bohm wasn't satisfied, and he thought hard about the implications of these paradoxical aspects of quantum mechanics.

Let me say a few words about these paradoxes. One of them is that in quantum mechanics we seem not to be able to describe what goes on in a fully deterministic way; in other words, we seem not to be able to explain what goes on in mechanistic detail. The second kind of paradox is that separate regions of space seem to be connected together in ways which one cannot readily understand in an ordinary kind of mental picture. Bohm, trying to understand these things, came up initially with the idea of hidden variables. What he proposed is that the fact that things don't seem to be well determined in science means that there are variables which we can't observe directly, which do, however, affect the physics. His views gradually evolved, and what he says now is that what these paradoxes show is the existence of an unmanifest or implicate order which we can't observe directly, and phenomena are created from this order rather in the same sort of way in which a cloud condenses from moist air. We see order in the observed phenomena which is the result of the unobserved order.

Thus Bohm views quantum mechanics as providing an indication that there is unobserved order in Nature. This now connects back to what I was saying much earlier on in my lecture, i.e., that if we want to put God into science, then we have to say that there is an intelligence behind the scenes which is creating order or at least leaving things less disordered than they would have been without the intelligence being present. And so we can identify the unobserved order with intelligence. Here we are on the way to the beginnings of a mathematical synthesis. If what Bohm is doing with unmanifest order can be combined with the mathematics of intelligence, we'll be well on the way to integrating God and his domain into the framework of science.

Now I'd like to go on from this to something which is quite speculative but which, I think, is indicated by the evidence. It is a correlation between the details of physics and the details of reality revealed by, e.g., the meditative experience. The correspondence is indicated in Table 1.

The ordinary reality as perceived by the senses corresponds to classical physics. The subtler realities of the astral or celestial worlds correspond to the aspect of physical reality described by quantum physics. Finally Bohm's unmanifest or implicate order corresponds to transcendental experience. These three experiential realities are experienced successively as one goes deeper into meditation. At first the mind concerns itself mainly with the ordinary aspects of life.

Table 1: Correspondence Between Physical Reality and Subjective Experiences

Physical Reality	Subjective Experiences
Classical physics	World of sensory experience
Quantum physics	Celestial worlds
Unmanifest order	Transcendental experience

Then deeper, non ordinary experiences occur. Ultimately, these give way in turn to the silent, peaceful, free from any specific identifiable content (and hence, like the order postulated by Bohm, unmanifest), transcendental experience. Going back one step, the celestial worlds are only partly real; their status, according to mysticism, is that of fantasy or possibility, which reminds us of the possibility or potentiality aspects of the quantum wave function. I would like to suggest here an actual identity behind the parallelism.

The picture one gets from sources like the *Vedas* is that our own intelligence is not something which is entirely within us: our inspirations and so on come from a different world, the celestial world. And this in turn is influenced by the absolute (or by God). So, to summarize, one can sketch out very roughly what the new kind of science, in which God is one of the actors, might look like. At the center we have this highest level of control, which would be conceived of as a very much more ideal and powerful version of our own intelligence. It would correspond to Bohm's unmanifest order, and would have profound influences on nature in fact, the whole structure of quantum mechanics, in Bohm's model, is

> *"...we might hope that appropriate mathematical tools will be developed, so that in not too many years from now we'll have a new paradigm in which God and religion will be right in the middle of the picture..."*

the result of the presence of this unmanifest order and so the way we viewed science would be different. We would say really the whole structure of science, once we get to the quantum level (where the unmanifest order makes observable order), would be directly the result of God's presence and works. I must add that this is my own interpretation of the theory; Bohm doesn't necessarily agree with this interpretation (or disagree with it). And we might hope that appropriate mathematical tools will be developed, so that in not too many years from now we'll have a new paradigm in which God and religion will be right in the middle of the picture, instead of being pushed out almost entirely as is the case at the present time.

SCIENCE IN THE THIRD MILLENNIUM:
EXPECTATIONS BETWEEN HOPE AND FEAR
Richard R. Ernst

Nobel Laureate in Chemistry, Zurich, Switzerland

The turn of a millennium has certainly a special appeal. We believe, so to say, to hear the eternal clock ticking. Possibly, we become aware that we are involved in an evolutionary process that we might very well adversely influence, but which we cannot stop nor reverse. Whatever we have done, good or bad, will remain with us, or without us, for eternity. I can understand that certain philosophies and religions have introduced the notion of merits which determine our destiny, our salvation, or perhaps for some believers, our beneficial rebirth.

1. Our Two Souls

We scientists know in principle that there is only action and reaction, cause and effect. We are convinced that we can explain the course of events with rational reasoning alone. We do not need the mystery of all these myriads of deities, of demons, *dharmapālas, bodhisattvas,* and *avatāras.* We are relying exclusively on the eternal laws of nature which can be formulated mathematically, and which form the basis of all conceivable matter and fields. We know all that is ever needed to be known to explain the world, and if not, we are capable of discovering the yet unknown laws.

On the occasion of the turn of the millennium, a revealing book has been published, *Predictions for the Next Millennium* by David Kristof and Todd W. Nickerson (1998) with the thoughts of two hundred and seventy contemporaries on the future thousand years of human evolution. I will frequently add citations from this fascinating volume during my lecture. Let me start with the prediction of Herbert A. Hauptman, Nobel Prize winner in Chemistry in 1985:

"Hope for the future - That the people of the world will at long last come to recognize that the universe is a realization of a logical structure permitting a rational description, that there is no place for belief in the supernatural, and that no evidence exists for belief in an all knowing, all powerful intelligence."

But are we so sure? Many of us scientists lead a rather strange double life: rational at work and emotional at home. Perhaps being at the same time a successful manager of a computer company and a leading member of a fundamentalist religious group, carrying not only two hats, but apparently also two brains and two souls, the public one and the private one.

Why do I mention this here? Perhaps, it is because we Westerners see here in India the disparity of the two worlds more clearly than in our own countries where we can better hide the conflicts. Our second life proceeds behind impenetrable walls, and we do not let our private soul parade on the streets, while here in India, all aspects of life are fully apparent already on the marketplace. Some of us also try to find here in India, or in the East in general, a counterpart with whom our private soul can resonate and by whom it may be nourished, being on a starvation diet in the west. India is considered, so to say, as the place where ladders to happiness and eternity can be rented.

I think only when we find possibilities to harmonize and unify our logical and our spiritual basis (if I am allowed to employ this often misused term), we will be in a position to fulfil the tasks and obligations of the future.

We should be aware that there is a true schism between science and society. They form so-to-say two disparate worlds. On the one hand, there is society claiming that science is responsible for most of the evil on earth, having caused all the pollution, Bhopal, Seveso, and Chernobyl, a society that is nevertheless thoughtlessly using and misusing all the goodies of science and technology.

On the other hand, there are many of our great achievers in science who still think in terms of unlimited progress on a technological level. They are convinced that progress of mankind is measured in our ability to conquer outer space, to colonize in a not too far future the moon and some of the planets of our solar system, to extend the living time of individuals, and to genetically modify man in order to extinguish the martial traits in his character. Science will solve all conceivable problems. Let me present a few citations to underline my point, without implying that these cursory remarks represent the ultimate opinion of their authors:

Sir Derek H. R. Barton (1969 Nobel Prize for Chemistry): "I predict that Molecular Biologists will find out how to stop the aging process. We can then live forever. The world population will grow ad infinitum. A real problem!" (- but the true problems facing us he seems to have missed!)

Michael S. Brown (1985 Nobel Prize for Medicine): "In the third millennium the greatest challenge to humanity will emerge from the ability to control by chemical means the thought process of human beings." - hard to believe that this will be the greatest challenge!

Glenn T. Seaborg (1951 Nobel Prize for Chemistry): "Drugs that will improve intelligence."- as if the lack of intelligence would be our worst deficiency!

This is the kind of reasoning we are often taught in our universities. We acquire scientific and analytical skills. We become fascinated and creative inventors and explorers. We discover incredible possibilities of understanding and exploiting nature, and we lay the foundation for a plethora of useful and enjoyable gadgets and tools. We become convinced that we are truly indispensable for maintaining and improving the standard of living of our society and for keeping our free market economy running at full speed.

Is it really a meaningful goal to further improve the standard of living of an affluent minority and to extend their individual life span? Wouldn't it be better to attempt to extend the life span of the entire mankind on earth? If we do not think long-term, nature will find its own ways to set limits: 'Eat and be eaten!' If we do not think far ahead, our descendants will have to experience the fatal limits without being properly prepared. We might hope that the fatal consequences of our doing will not hit us and will become active only generations later. Who should care about the far future? "Après nous le déluge!" said Madame de Pompadour (1721-1764), the favorite courtisanne of Louis XV of France. And in some way, it makes sense: Why should we care? We are ourselves accidental products of nature and are not responsible for our existence. We should give life a meaning by enjoying it at every moment. Why should we worry about the future? Anyway we can not control earthquakes nor typhoons! Nor can we trust our dishonest politicians who might destroy our future.

2. Sustainable Development

This leads us to the question of sustainability. The principle of sustainable development is today a well accepted conversation piece in any upper class society, as long as it concerns the behavior of our neighbor and not our own. Why should we not drive with our own car to pick up some less expensive goods produced in a country with less environmental regulation? After all, we are living in a free market economy! It is anyway the task of science to develop sustainable procedures that allow us to continue our life style without increased costs, without conflicting with our beloved shareholder value thinking. That is why society pays decent salaries to the scientists at public institutions!

Let us hear five alarming voices, contradicting this shortsighted view:

Steingrimur Hermannsson (Former Prime Minister of Iceland): "Hopefully, Man will soon enough come to realize that he will not survive on Earth without a healthy environment and a biological diversity. Hopefully, Man will have the wisdom and courage to discontinue his devastating behavior and repair some of the damages that have been made. If not, I fear a catastrophe."

Judd Hirsch (TV, film and Broadway actor): "If this space age, this latter second millennium, has taught us anything, it is that we live on a fragile planet with an onionskin atmosphere, containing all that is dear to natural life. And that we humans are rapidly turning all of it to waste, including even the narrowest band of breathable air, at an alarming rate of pollution, destruction and overpopulation. And if we have learned anything significant from the first two millenniums, it would be that we only have a tiny fraction of the third millennium to change it. I only wish I could predict we shall!"

Douglas D. Osheroff (1996 Nobel Prize for Physics): "If man does not learn to control population growth by more benign means, disease and famine will limit the human population to roughly twelve billion persons."

Jerome Karle (1985 Nobel Prize for Chemistry): "If humans continue to increase the earth's population, destroy the environment and produce children whose lives are devoid of love, self-respect, culture and respect for the dignity of all others, we can expect an increasing loss of quality of life, much suffering and violence, and a return to dark ages. If these current, self destructive, large-scale assaults on our earth and its societies are sufficiently curtailed, science, technology and widespread rational thought and ethics should be able to bring the quality of life to unprecedented, high levels."

Robert S. McNamara (Former US secretary of defense): "I believe that the indefinite combination of human fallibility and nuclear weapons will lead to destruction of nations. Therefore, I predict the next millennium will witness either nuclear catastrophe or the elimination of nuclear weapons."

Coming back to my previous comment about the distrustful politicians, I am convinced that the major crime against sustainability is the one on moral grounds. If we cannot trust each other anymore, we and our future are lost forever. We will have no chance to implement the necessary measures.

3. Science and Ethics

I am convinced that by purely rational thinking, based on the value-free laws of science, we cannot find ultimate solutions and we cannot create a lasting global order that prevents violent conflicts. Let me cite the prediction of Hal Prince that fits into this context:

Hal Prince (Broadway productions producer): "Our current obsession with technology is a dead end - unless the next Millennium renews our faith in the unknown - the miraculous mystery of Man's Soul."

Science and technology alone cannot solve the problems of the new millennium. We need additional guidelines for our actions, for the selection of our research projects and research goals. These guidelines have to do with ethics, with philosophy, and with faith. We do not have to reinvent ethics. Our ethical systems already have a many thousand years old tradition. They are the lasting foundations of human civilization. These value systems are or have been imbedded in a liturgical context of very varied forms, ranging from very elementary, animistic and schamanistic manifestations to highly sophisticated, esoteric and intellectual edifices.

"Science and technology alone cannot solve the problems of the new millennium. We need additional guidelines for our actions, for the selection of our research projects and research goals. These guidelines have to do with ethics, with philosophy, and with faith."

Many of us scientists have a split and ambivalent relation to the spiritual aspects of existence. Some of us are completely disinterested in religion and spirituality, and refuse to even think about these subjects. Others are pronounced atheists, finding only contradictions between belief and knowledge. A few are true agnostics claiming that a proof of the existence of supernatural forces is forever out of our reach. And, finally, many scientists lead truly a double life, adhering to a rather simple-minded belief on Sunday and acting in a strictly rational manner on weekdays. While the total rejection of religious considerations is more frequent in Europe, many American scientists and nonscientific citizens are subjected to the mentioned schism. Just watch for a few hours American TV and you will realize what I am speaking about.

Reading about eastern religions, about Hinduism and Buddhism, which I know particularly in its Tibetan Lamaistic form, and its form of Zen Buddhism, I came to the conclusion that these philosophies can more easily be amalgamated with our scientific edifice. The ethical principles behind and also some of the religious concepts are more open-minded to be combined with other systems of value. They appear to be less exclusive than our western monotheistic religions, which have led and are still leading to cruel religious wars. Indeed, I have found many Indians and Japanese scientists who are perhaps more mature personalities than can easily be found among western scientists. But unfortunately, I had to learn that these sages also form a very small minority, and the rest tries to imitate our Western superficiality. The knowledge of historical religions and philosophies is often quite meager also in Asia, although some superficial traditional rituals may still be obeyed in their daily life, often perhaps more due to convenience and opportunism than to personal conviction. After all, why should one not take advantage of the pre-established privileges provided by a traditional society?

Why do I put so much emphasis on the schism between science and the spiritual aspects of life? The reason for this is my conviction that even more important than further support of pure and detached science is to achieve an integration of the two apparently diverging aspects. It is hard to believe that the enormous scientific and technological development of the past two hundred years should have no influence on our ethical system of values. It is even harder to believe that three to four thousand years of philosophical and religious development should not deeply influence our attitude towards nature, and science and technology. I am convinced that we all are called to devote part of our mental efforts to achieve progress in the direction of establishing a unified ethical system of values which may serve as a basis for a future beneficial development of science and society on a global scale.

> "I am convinced that we all are called to devote part of our mental efforts to achieve progress in the direction of establishing a unified ethical system of values which may serve as a basis for a future beneficial development of science and society on a global scale."

I do not think that this task is easy. I do not even think that it can be completed, once and for ever. It rather marks a process than an achievable goal, a process which will occupy mankind for as long as it will exist. We should not hope for an ingenious inventor of a new system. We have many discouraging examples in the past where individuals or small groups of intellectuals tried to create revolutionary novel rules for society. Certainly the most prominent examples are Marx and Engels laying the foundations of communism. But we might also mention the Islamic Republic in Iran, the Talibans in Afghanistan, and the cultural revolution in China, initiated by Mao and his clique. This is certainly not the way to proceed. What we need is not a new set of dogmatic absolute laws, but rather a flexible ethical foundation with very basic concepts which are not in conflict with more exclusive humanistic traditions nor with modern science.

I would just like to advocate that we engrave into our brain the need for such a development, and that we actively undertake considerations into this direction. I would like to propose to include in scientific congresses and meetings, sessions, lectures, or discussion groups on ethical issues of science and society. The scientific community should actively contribute towards a renewed ethical basis of a technology and science-supported global society.

I am convinced that the Indian science community has, in this regard, a very essential role to play. India is in a unique position in many respects:

(i) India is the source of some of the most profound schools of thought of mankind with the *Mahābhārata* and the *Bhagavadgītā* expressing Hindu philosophy and the *Tripiṭaka* summarizing the Buddhist view. Both philosophical systems with their respect for all beings and expression of compassion may be fruitful sources for a universal ethical system.

(ii) India is a universe by itself, not only in numbers of population, but also being in parts an ultramodern computerized country, and in other parts showing all signs of a developing, partly even medieval country with virtually all conceivable problems of a traditional society exposed to the influences of modern industrialism. An ethical system that works in India should work everywhere else as well.

(iii) India has a well developed academic community with a surplus of highly creative scientists, perhaps with a special inclination towards the more theoretical aspects of science and maintaining still a link to the ancient Indian culture.

I am convinced that India could become once again the cradle of a new school of thoughts that may significantly influence the fate of the globe during the third millennium. Perhaps the contributions of India to nuclear power technology and space science will turn out to be irrelevant, but the contribution towards a new ethical foundation could be turning the wheel of history in the proper direction.

> *"Perhaps the contributions of India to nuclear power technology and space science will turn out to be irrelevant, but the contribution towards a new ethical foundation could be turning the wheel of history in the proper direction."*

I certainly do not want to advocate that the scientists should stop doing research and spend all their time contemplating on ethics and philosophy of life. Perhaps, you remember the ancient Hindu role model for a high-caste male, a model that probably has seldom been practiced to its full extent. Life is supposed to consist of four stages:

(i) As a student, one is learning from a knowledgeable teacher.

(ii) As a householder, one is founding a family and is active in society, industry, or academics.

(iii) As a forest dweller, one retreats with the wife into the forests, meditates on the world and tries to make sense out of the previous experiences, and seeks ones own release from the world.

(iv) As a *sannyāsī*, finally, one leaves everything, including the wife behind and wanders as a beggar throughout the country, meditating, and seeking to achieve a state of mind that transcends the world.

Obviously, this model is hard to follow in our time. Where would you find all the necessary forests? But still, it neatly summarizes our tasks in life. In principle, it is phase (iii) which serves the purpose of advancing the ethical foundations. But today, we rather have to spend the spare time during our active period (ii) for this purpose. Obviously, it is better to adopt a trial and error procedure during the active life instead of realizing too late what has gone wrong during our period (ii).

I would like to add a few citations from the mentioned book to underline my points:

Arun Gandhi (Gandhi Institute for Nonviolence): "Out of the ashes of materialism will rise the spectre of true morality and meaning of life. There will be greater compassion towards humans and nature by the year 3000."

Helmut Schmidt (Former German Chancellor): "The new century would be blessed if all of us would more than hitherto stress and live up to the moral principle of any human being's responsibility."

Lech Walesa (1983 Nobel Peace Prize) "Settling the issues of religious dimensions of man."

Elie Wiesel (1986 Nobel Peace Prize) "Less fanaticism. More compassion for children. More solidarity with victims of illness and injustice."

Phil Collins (Famous rock musician) "We have to learn to understand our fellow man and be considerate of his beliefs and religion. Without this we will self-destruct."

Perhaps, you have heard of the Student Pugwash USA movement which calls for ethics in science. It has on an Internet page (http://www.igc.org/pugwash/pledge.html) a pledge which one may sign in order to accept some personal commitment. Perhaps, it might influence your own behavior, although nobody checks on it.

4. Virtues of Scientists

I would like to emphasize three basic properties that a scientist in our time should possess in order to be able to properly fulfil his obligations:

(i) **Curiosity**: Without a vital curiosity, creative scientific work is impossible. It is normally considered as the source of inspiration and the drive to work day and night without an adequate payment per hour. In principle, everybody has an inborn curiosity and is in this regard a scientist. Without our curiosity, mankind would never have become what it is today. Scientists are just professional explorers who have perfected this human drive.

(ii) **Honesty and Self-critics**: The most important property of a scientist is unlimited honesty. Without honesty, incorrectly describing experiments and results, science loses its right of existence. A scientist might survive without being creative or without mathematical skills. But he should be immediately executed if he is dishonest and does not admit it. Cheating on scientific results is about the worst a scientist can do. You know that even more dangerous than cheating your neighbor is cheating yourself because then there is no way out of the mess anymore. It is like the impossibility of pulling yourself out of the mud by your own hair.

Scientists are making errors, naturally, they are human beings, and achieving results that last rock-solid forever is illusionary. A scientist has to be able to question his own ingenious results, even his own person, daily, constantly. Self-criticism is a very important scientific property. No honest scientist should stick rigidly to his own overaged ideas. Flexibility in imagining alternative explanations of natural phenomena is essential. Doing science can indeed be very painful, and abandoning previous, seemingly spectacular achievements happens every day.

(iii) **Responsibility**: Scientists often request unlimited freedom in the selection and pursuit of their research projects. True, without liberty, one cannot find anything new, and scientific endeavors become meaningless. The scientists themselves have to find the relevant problems to work on. The 'bottom-up approach' is the proper one, and not the 'top-down approach' where political committees decide about the direction that science should take. This would just lead to activity but to little productivity, perhaps a good way to get rid of the anyway much too limited research funds but certainly not an avenue to obtain relevant results.

I would like to make a relevant point, "freedom means responsibility". Those who are granted freedom have to deliberately do what has to be done. They are supposed to find out what is needed and to orient their activities accordingly. Meaningful research cannot be done in the ivory tower but has to relate in some way to reality and to the needs of society.

In this sense, there is no pure science. All science is in some, at least remote way applied. I normally reject the distinction between pure or basic and applied science. Just the time lag of a practical application might differ. Even scientists in as abstract fields such as number theory or elementary particle theory should constantly think about the practical relevance of their research.

Obviously, research funding agencies should not ask for immediate social benefit of research projects. They, as well as the scientists, have to look far ahead into the future. And also the possibility of failures in the prediction of usefulness has to be taken into account. Without risk, there will be no success.

Honesty and responsibility also call for certain restraints in the promotion of trendy, spectacular projects that bring little profit. The public is often misled by overstressing the importance of interplanetary missions. Very little information is obtained by a Mars landing and from microphones deposited on a dead planet.

On one of our Swissair flight from Zurich to Mumbai, we met a flight attendant who had successfully founded in Mumbai a school for deserving street children in Mumbai, for deserving children who had not found access to the regular schools. For me, these helpers are the real heroes of our time and not the engineers who want to build an Indian moon rocket which hardly solves any one of the urgent problems. To speak with the words of Arundhati Roy: "However many garlands we heap on our scientists, however many medals we pin to their chests, the truth is that it's far easier to make a (atomic) bomb than to educate four hundred million people". Sometime ago, Arundhati Roy was arrested near the Narmada river project, a project which appears to disregard the needs of the poorest of the poor.

One might ask whether in a country like India, is it better to support research at the current international research front, although the results might be of little direct relevance for the country, or whether acting responsibly requires research more oriented towards the needs of the country. No simple yes/no answer can be given. Obviously, some scientists might prefer international fame to local recognition, and it is indeed necessary to remain at the forefront of science to be taken seriously. But there is not just one single international research front, and some fronts are more relevant for India than others. Each research group should select projects where it has a significant advantage in comparison with the competitors.

And who is in a better position to solve problems that relate to the Indian society, industry, and environment? By contributing towards the development of India, science also gains international relevance and recognition, because a stable and prosperous India is of enormous importance for the entire world.

I was quite excited to read a highly relevant leading article in Science magazine, November 12, 1999 issue, written by one of the internationally most respected Indian scientists, C.N.R.Rao: "Unfortunately, it is becoming increasingly difficult for Indian researchers who work at the cutting edge of science and technology to do their jobs well because of poor infrastructure and facilities at most institutions, in particular the universities. As a result, the gap in the level of science and technology between advanced countries and India is increasing". I support his view of science in developing countries that also applies to some developed countries. He ends with the strong statement: "It is only by making use of a strong knowledge base that India can ever hope to become a great nation." This very clear article should be framed and posted by all scientists and concerned science administrators in the government.

"It is only by making use of a strong knowledge base that India can ever hope to become a great nation."

— C. N. R. Rao

Perhaps, scientists should go more into politics. Their combination of knowledge, honesty, responsibility, international cooperation, and hopefully also compassion makes them predestinate to carry political responsibility. I am convinced that the political situation on earth could not suffer from more involvement of scientists.

Any scientist has two obligations: creative research and academic teaching. But in fact, there is a third obligation of at least equal importance. You know that the survival of mankind in prosperity and decency does not so much depend on us scientists than on the proper behavior of society in general and the politicians in particular. It is not the task of science to solve the problems of a thoughtless society spoiling resources and our environment. It is not the scientists who have to invent tricks so that the population can continue its desired luxurious life style not thinking about the consequences for the future. On the contrary, if our population and its leaders do not know how to behave responsibly, the living ground of science will also be destroyed.

The remedies to be taken are clear. Because we believe to have recognized the inherent dangers and we have at least some partial answers, it is our responsibility to educate and to inform society. This is our third and perhaps most important obligation. Whenever we see a possibility to address our citizens, we should take the opportunity to enhance their knowledge so that they can properly judge themselves how good or bad their actions are in view of the future of themselves and their offsprings. We have to present public lectures, write popular articles, speak at radio stations, and appear in front of television. It is a demanding and time-consuming obligation that requires the efforts of all scientists, an enormous task when you consider the size of the Indian population. We cannot delegate this obligation to a few professional mediators. We have to do it ourselves, better today than tomorrow.

5. My Second Stage of Life

Making reference to the Indian model of the four stages of life, I myself have just entered the third stage after my retirement a year ago. Sometimes, I am looking back at my performance during my second, the active stage of life.

From the beginning, I had two goals in mind: First, I was looking for exciting research in a field where mathematical modelling and understanding was feasible, and second, I wanted to achieve something useful for mankind. My first goal had its origin in my fear of people. I wanted to work undisturbed in a laboratory for myself. The second goal had to do with my lacking self-esteem. I needed confirmation of my own usefulness by a significant contribution to society. And indeed, I was enormously lucky. The field into which I was pushed by my thesis advisor, nuclear magnetic resonance, was enormously fascinating and intellectually challenging, and after all it turned out to be of surprising usefulness. I achieved in my life more than I ever wanted to achieve. I think I was just very lucky, and I do not claim any credit for my performance.

Nuclear magnetic resonance (NMR) was originally conceived as an esoteric physical technique for exploring nuclear properties by Edward Purcell and Felix Bloch in 1945. The discovery of the chemical shifts in 1950, where the resonance frequencies of the nuclei are influenced by the surrounding electron density, allowed one to use the nuclei as sensors or spies to examine chemical properties of molecules. However, sensitivity of the method was very low, and only simple molecules could be investigated. The introduction of Fourier transform spectroscopy in 1964 by W.A. Anderson and myself changed the situation. Sensitivity was enhanced by two orders of magnitude, and applications in molecular biology became feasible. With the advent of two-dimensional spectroscopy, suggested for the first time by Jean Jeener in 1971, it became possible to determine protein and nucleic acid structures in solution. About the same time, Paul Lauterbur introduced magnetic resonance imaging which became of major clinical importance in medicine for the non-invasive diagnosis of many types of diseases. My own contributions were invariably associated with Fourier transformation and the resulting increase in the information flux. Today, NMR is probably the most informative technique with an universal applicability ranging from physics, to chemistry, biology, and medicine.

Obviously, this spectacular development, taking place during my active stage of life, gave me great satisfaction.

6. Conclusions

Certainly, the importance of science will not diminish during the third millennium. At first, science is needed for supporting a still growing world population by developing technologies which cause a minimal load on the environment and allowing for an extended period of human existence. Secondly, science has the continuing obligation to teach and instruct the population about environmentally adequate behavior which is perhaps even more important than the first task. Finally, science has to make its own contribution to the development of a new global ethics that overcomes the all too apparent pitfalls of our free market economy which might soon run into a dead end.

There is a principle of self-fulfilling prophecy. We need a positive attitude towards development in the future. This is a necessary condition for a good outcome. But it is by no means a sufficient one. We have to change a lot in our behavior as scientists, as individuals, as members of communities, as members of states, and as parts of a global human culture. We have most likely to significantly modify our economic system, and we have to find a renewed ethical foundation of our relations towards our fellow citizens and towards nature. These relations should be founded on tolerance, compassion, and respect more than ever before.

Let me end with my own prediction, found in the same book:

"After the first millennium of the municipal communities and the second one of the nations, we will enter a third millennium of the global communities. Conflicts will no longer be settled between nations but between social groupings, between the haves and the have-nots. The fights for survival might become increasingly cruel and costly.

"The free market system will have to be severely modified with penalties taking into account all adverse side effects. Numerous variations of a constrained global market system will be tried out, most of them leading deeper and deeper into economical and ecological disasters, until, finally, a self-regulating system will be found that allows for an almost unlimited survival of mankind, although with drastically reduced population numbers, living standard, and individual freedom.

"Hopefully, our present excessive materialistic wealth will be replaced by a wealth of cultural creativity and productivity. However, a self-induced disaster that wipes out all previous cultural achievements is not inconceivable either."

Finally, the words of Edward Albee, the famous American playwriter, point possibly into our next life:

"Maybe we can do better next time!"

If not we ourselves, then hopefully, our children and grandchildren will learn from our mistakes.

DIALOGUE ON LIFE AND ITS ORIGIN
University of Basel, Switzerland

Professor Werner Arber (right), a Nobel Laureate and Emeritus Professor of Molecular Biology greets Dr. T. D. Singh (His Holiness Bhaktisvarūpa Dāmodara Swami), Director of the Bhaktivedanta Institute and President of the Vedanta and Science Educational Research Foundation, Kolkata, at the University of Basel, Switzerland.

Dr. T. D. Singh (henceforth TDS): Professor Arber, I am very pleased to see you here in Switzerland. You are respected throughout the world for your great contribution to the life sciences as well as for your concern for the welfare of humanity. Switzerland is a very beautiful country. Its landscapes, mountains, lakes and people are all extremely impressive. I came here on the invitation of a friend of mine, Mr. Claude Bolay. Unfortunately he had passed away only ten days before I reached here.

Professor Werner Arber (henceforth WA): Oh, is that so?

TDS: Yes. It is very sad. I condoled with his family members. They were happy that I came here to see them. Life is really uncertain. Mr. Bolay had a sincere and keen desire to seek the deeper and spiritual meaning of life. This common interest brought us closer.

I am not an expert in life sciences. But due to my background in chemistry and the Vedantic tradition[1] of India, I have a deep interest in the scientific and philosophical search for the understanding of life and its origin. Today, most chemical evolutionists[2] and molecular biologists strongly proclaim that life is an evolutionary product of well-organized complex molecular reactions. It seems to me that they claim too much with too few scientific facts. I sincerely feel that the question of life is related not only to science, but also to philosophy and theology. And thus, I think that a deeper dialogue on life is very necessary.

WA: Yes, right.

TDS: While looking into some of the literatures, I find that some of your thoughts regarding life and its origin are very interesting. Your view is different from most of the other molecular biologists and evolutionary chemists. I have been waiting for an opportunity to discuss with you some of the scientific and philosophical questions about life and I feel very happy that we are meeting now.

First of all, molecular evolutionists[3] around the globe are trying very hard to simulate the atmospheric chemical reactions in the hope of generating various chemical steps going from simple to complex biomolecules in the laboratory. They hope that this type of research may lead to the production of a primordial living cell in the laboratory.

However, it seems to me that these studies may not be so necessary because we already have the know-how and techniques to isolate practically all the biomolecules from existing living bodies. Hence, we can start with these ready-made biomolecules instead of starting from simpler molecules at immense expense of time, manpower and finances. Somehow or other if we can assemble these biomolecules in a reaction flask it could be possible to tell, whether or not life is a product of the combination of these biomolecules. Chemical evolutionists often claim that given a cosmic time scale or a long time span, life could generate spontaneously from the assembly of these molecules. However, if we can find a super-catalyst or a super-enzyme, then the problem of a long time span will be solved. That would be more reasonable than doing research on how small molecules would become big molecules, for example, from amino acids to protein molecules, which in turn might or might not lead to the first primordial living cell. Scientists in this field can design some research work on how to find some special enzymes[4] in order to accelerate these chemical reactions. I would appreciate your opinion in this regard.

WA: Of course, we can accelerate the chemical reactions by having appropriate enzymes. But the manifestation of life is much deeper than that. For me, I think the mystery of life is still to conceive how these

> *"...I think that life could be beyond the assembly of biomolecules."*
> — Werner Arber

organic molecules, which are already similar or equal to what we know today to represent components of organic life, come together such that some living primordial cell may become functioning. This, I don't understand. So, that is a difficult problem. In addition, I think that life could be beyond the assembly of biomolecules. For a number of years I had concentrated on exploring molecular evolution, and I had also raised questions on the origin of life which is of wide interest. But, I have given up trying to find answers to these latter questions. I know how difficult it is. However, many scientists still think that the properties of matter, organic molecules, are such that life could be a probable event. I guess the question is: how probable will that be?

TDS: It seems to me that we cannot all agree even over the definition of life. Molecular evolutionists define life as complex molecular reactions whereas spiritualists describe life as a divine spark.

WA: Yes. Well, this is not so easy.

TDS: If we take the religious or spiritual viewpoint, especially the Vedic viewpoint, there are two principles of reality, the material realm and the spiritual realm. Physics and chemistry are within the first category whereas life belongs to the nonphysical spiritual realm and it follows its own spiritual laws.

WA: Oh, it is not so easily accessible. I don't know. I work with microorganisms, mainly bacteria. I guess you generally believe in the existence of a spiritual soul. With which organisms does that start? Is it limited to human beings only?

TDS: Yes, I do believe in the existence of a non-chemical or non-molecular spiritual soul. We all agree that the living bodies are made up of organic matter, molecules. But according to the Vedic science, these bodies are animated by the presence of the soul, just like the analogy of a car and the driver inside. When the driver goes away, the car cannot move. Similarly, when the spirit soul goes away, or what we call death, the body can no longer be animated in spite of the fact that all the molecular machineries that make up the body are still intact.

According to the spiritual paradigm contained in Vedanta[5], the seed of life, the spiritual soul, has been existing since eternity and life manifests itself from the very moment of conception at least in higher living beings, such as human beings.

In Vedic cosmology, there are periodic cycles known as *yuga* cycles and creation and annihilation of the material world along with living beings take place continuously like changes of seasons. There are four *yugas* in each *yuga* cycle namely, *Satya*, *Tretā*, *Dvāpara* and *Kali* and the seeds of life are injected by the Supreme Lord into the womb of material nature. When the appropriate cosmic cycle appears, many different biological forms manifest in that particular *yuga* cycle. Also according to Vedanta, since all biological forms have already been existing in subtle states, either manifested or unmanifested, embodied life on earth would start, in principle, from any organism — bacteria, plants, birds, animals, human beings, etc., according to the subtle laws of *karma*[6]. The word *karma* is a Sanskrit word and it means the action – both psychological and physical - performed by the living entity under the influence of the three modes of material nature (*guṇas*).

Vedic cosmology or Vedantic cosmology supports the simultaneous manifestation of many organisms. This principle is in direct contradiction with the Darwinian paradigm. If the existence of the soul is recognized in Darwinian paradigm then the spiritual paradigm of Vedanta could integrate the Darwinian paradigm. Thus the missing element in neo-Darwinian paradigm or molecular biology is the spiritual soul. However, in vedantic paradigm, consciousness evolves and the biological forms are designed in such a way that each form can accommodate the evolving conscious level of the living entity. This process is also known as the transmigration of the soul.

So, according to the spiritual paradigm of Vedic science the presence of the spirit soul is not limited to human beings only. However, we should note that some religious traditions do not accept the existence of the soul and some others proclaim that the soul is present in human beings only. The ancient Vedic science of India does not accept such statements. Rather the Vedic science states very firmly that all living entities have spirit souls.

WA: All living entities?

TDS: Yes, all living entities including microorganisms.

WA: That sounds quite interesting.

TDS: Professor Arber, it is extremely fascinating to read your work on the discovery and use of restriction enzymes. You explain that restriction enzymes are protein molecules that cut deoxyribonucleic acid (DNA) chains. During an attack of an invading bacteriophage, the bacterium releases a so-called restriction enzyme that recognizes the DNA of the invading bacteriophage and cuts the DNA into pieces, thereby disabling it. Simultaneously, the bacterium releases another enzyme that defends and protects its own DNA from being cut by the restriction enzyme. It seems that even microorganisms have some sort of built-in intelligent system, which would indicate that life displays unique qualities even at the level of microorganisms. This restriction enzyme of a bacterium cuts the viral DNA of foreign origin to safeguard and preserve its own identity. What a beautiful system nature has! Can you elaborate on this?

WA: If the DNA of a bacterium invades a cell of another strain of bacteria, the restriction enzymes of the infected bacterium recognizes that DNA as of a foreign origin. That could also be a viral DNA if it had been grown in another type of bacteria. The way to identify this is that bacteria usually mark their own DNA in a strain-specific nucleotide[7] sequence by methylation. Methylation of a DNA base is accomplished by methylation enzymes. Thus, it is the methyl group ($-CH_3$) in a specific sequence context that serves as a tag for the distinction between own and foreign. If an invading DNA molecule is identified as foreign, restriction enzymes will cut it into fragments which are then a substrate[8] for further degradation. However, with some low probability, a segment of DNA can find a chance to recombine with the cellular DNA. That is an essential step in the natural horizontal transfer[9] of genetic information from one type of bacteria to another. I call that the acquisition strategy. Of course, if this would happen too often, it would not be good. The bacterial population would lose its genetic stability. I think it is important that there is a natural defense mechanism. So, most attempts to bring in foreign DNA are not successful because of the restriction. But in small steps, segments of foreign DNA are sometimes accepted. For me, this is a very good way for a strain of bacteria to acquire novel genetic information which is available elsewhere. We must be aware, however, that such acquisition does not occur in nature in a reflected way. Rather, it happens largely at random.

TDS: The interesting principle is that the bacterium also releases another enzyme to protect its own DNA. It does not destroy its own DNA by the restriction enzyme.

WA: No, indeed, it protects its own DNA by methylation at proper sites within specific DNA sequences.

TDS: Can you explain the mechanism of how the bacterial cell can have such a built-in system to provide restriction as well as protection simultaneously? I think that this may have some important philosophical implication.

WA: Well, there are indeed philosophical aspects. I appreciate that you see this while many people don't. Actually, on the basis of

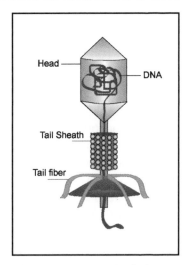

Figure 2.2: A typical T-even bacteriophage (virus that infects bacteria): It has a complex capsid consisting of a head and tail. DNA is stored in head and tail piece functions in the injection of this DNA into a bacterium.

Head — DNA

Tail Sheath

Tail fiber

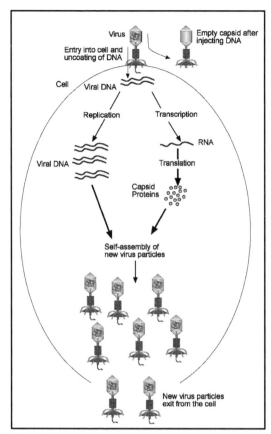

Figure 2.3: A simplified Viral Photocopying Mechanism: A virus uses the equipment of its host cell to make its copies. After entering the cell, the viral DNA uses host nucleotides and enzymes to reproduce itself and other hosts material and machinery to produce its capsid proteins. Viral DNA and capsid proteins then assemble to make new virus copies and then leave the cell.

these and many other properties of microorganisms, I have formulated, in a crude form, a theory of molecular evolution. This theory postulates that populations of living beings occasionally produce genetic variants by using three qualitatively different strategies. One is the gene acquisition strategy which we have already discussed. The second is a reshuffling of DNA segments within the genome[10]. This process is normally mediated by specific recombination enzymes. The third strategy is to generate genetic variants which bring about small local changes in the DNA sequences, such as the substitution of a nucleotide or the deletion or insertion of one or a few nucleotides.

These latter changes can occur upon DNA replication because of the limited stability of nucleotides. In literature, such local changes are often described as errors or mistakes. However, I consider this as an unfair interpretation of the observations. From my point of view, such local changes in DNA sequences are a direct consequence of the slight structural and chemical instability of the nucleotides.

TDS: So, you are saying that, contrary to the opinion of other scientists, mutation is not a mistake or an error in replication; it is a natural process. This is a significant observation.

WA: Yes, indeed. And nature uses that property in order to get some flexibility in the forms of life. Of course, without genetic variation you could not have any evolution, nor biodiversity. Interestingly, in all the three natural strategies of generation of genetic variations, the products of specific genes are involved. We call them evolution genes. Their products act as enzymes that mediate the reactions. Some of the enzymes directly act as generators of genetic variations, while others rather modulate the frequency of genetic variation. Note that the genetic variations of evolutionary relevance must be both non-reproducible from case to case and are relatively rare. The latter condition serves to insure a certain genetic stability to the species of organisms.

Let us come back to the biological function of restriction-modification systems in bacteria. As we have already discussed, the restriction enzymes cut foreign DNA into fragments when it penetrates into a bacterial cell. Occasionally, a DNA fragment escapes further degradation and finds a way to incorporate by recombination somewhere into the bacterial genome. Hence, restriction enzymes carry out both properties typical for evolution genes: they seriously reduce the probability of success in horizontal gene transfer and also provide the opportunity for gene acquisition in small steps. In taking the activities of all evolution genes together, we can realize that nature has succeeded in providing means for a steady evolution of life. Evolution does not occur on the basis of errors, accidents or the action of selfish genetic elements. Rather, the evolution genes must have been fine-tuned for their functions to provide and to replenish a wide diversity of life forms capable to cope with the very different conditions of life found on

> *"Evolution does not occur on the basis of errors, accidents or the action of selfish genetic elements. Rather, the evolution genes must have been fine-tuned for their functions to provide and to replenish a wide diversity of life forms..."*
>
> — Werner Arber

our planet. Another philosophical aspect is that evolution genes, which act at the level of populations, are and can only be present in the same genome as the genes whose products serve for the essential processes of the life of each individual.

TDS: I can relate evolution in terms of the interaction between the conscious living entity (spiritual soul) and organic matter. We are talking about the evolution of life, which already exists. Vedic science describes the evolution of consciousness and that consciousness is an inherent quality of life. I wonder, in any form of life, at what stage can we see the development of symptoms of a real living cell or life? How is it possible for organic matter to acquire conscious property at any stage of molecular evolution unless the organic matter already has an in-built fundamental spiritual element or seed of life? People call this nature. In this regard I feel that there may be some possibility of bringing in the concept of divine nature and the role of divinity in the living system.

According to the Vedantic tradition, there are two categories of knowledge, *parā vidyā*[11], spiritual knowledge and *aparā vidyā*[12], material knowledge. This concept is elaborately explained in the *Upaniṣads*[13], the philosophical portions of the *Vedas*[14]. Life belongs to the *parā* realm of reality whereas matter or organic matter belongs to *aparā* aspect of reality. The interaction between organic matter and the living entity forms the embodied being.

> *"How is it possible for organic matter to acquire conscious property at any stage of molecular evolution unless the organic matter already has an in-built fundamental spiritual element or seed of life?"*
>
> — T. D. Singh

The philosophical understanding of the interaction of life and matter can be explained in the *Bhāgavata* school by the doctrine of *acintya-bhedābheda-tattva*[15] (inconceivably different and non-different) of Śrī Caitanya Mahāprabhu. According to this doctrine, the living entities and matter are both energies of the Supreme Lord. The living entities are His primary (*parā*) potency and matter is His secondary (*aparā*) potency. This simultaneous distinction and non-difference has sprung by His inconceivable power.

As mentioned earlier, in the Vedic tradition there is a natural law called *karma*. The concept of *karma* is similar to that of action and reaction in Newton's Law. According to the Vedantic science, the law of *karma* and the material modes of nature – *sattva*, *rajas* and *tamas* – goodness, passion and ignorance - are responsible for biodiversity as well as for diversity in terms of levels of intelligence, degree of development of mind and consciousness of the embodied being within the same species. The wheels of *karma* are driven by the will and desire of the embodied being. The results of *karma* are singular and pointed and there cannot be any error in them just as you say that mutation is not an error.

You say that biodiversity is due to genetic variation caused by occasional process of natural mutation. If it is possible to bring in the divine principle in natural mutation, there will be some conceptual similarity between the law of *karma* and the cause of genetic variation by natural mutation in explaining biodiversity. However, the difference between your philosophy and Vedantic philosophy is that in the Vedantic tradition, it is the consciousness that evolves, not the bodies. The transfer of a conscious being from one form to another takes place according to its *karma*. It is called evolution of consciousness, and it will go on until the being reaches its pure divinity of existence. There is good and bad *karma* according to the proper or improper use of one's free will as a human being. This conception is beyond the scope of modern biological sciences.

WA: Yes. Certainly, these philosophical aspects of life are worthy to be considered, but appear to be inaccessible by today's science.

TDS: You are an authority on viruses. I have seen your statement that virus is not life whereas many other biologists say it is life. Some biologists even argue that it is a missing link between non-life and life. Do you have any further thought on this?

WA: Virus alone is not life. Actually, I consider viruses as evolutionary instruments. They help evolution of the organisms, for example, by transporting genetic information from one type of organism to any other. But, of course, the problem is that one might condemn natural processes with in-built duality for good and bad. In the case of a virus interacting with its host, the host population may be helped in its evolution, but infected individuals may suffer from pathogenicity[16]. Well, we have to live with that!

TDS: Viruses already have the genetic materials within them. Although viruses can destroy the host cells, can we conceive of studying the origin of life using the virus as the starting point?

WA: No, I don't believe so. Although viruses may appear as autonomous entities, they cannot expand without an appropriate host cell.

TDS: It seems to me that a host cell acts like a photocopying machine. When a viral particle enters a host living cell, many copies of the virus are made inside the cell and thus viruses are multiplied (see figures 2.2 and 2.3).

WA: Yes, but that is not sufficient for life. You know, it is like polymerase chain reaction[17] (PCR), which is an efficient method for generating practically unlimited copies of any segment of DNA. Sometimes PCR is referred to as "molecular photocopy". You need only primers[18], which are, of course, complementary to short segments of the DNA that you want to copy and you need an enzyme; then it works and you can amplify the DNA segment. But that is only DNA and DNA is not life.

TDS: In the study of molecular evolution, many scientists like Thomas R. Cech and Sidney Altman[19] discovered that RNA has the ability to act as both genes and enzymes. And many scholars propose that this property of RNA would offer a way around the "chicken-and-egg" problem in the early part of molecular evolution (genes needed enzymes and enzymes needed genes). Some scientists think "RNA World"[20] is the pathway between non-life and life. Do you have any comment on the "RNA World" in regard to molecular evolution and life's origin?

WA: Well, it is an important discovery of Thomas R. Cech and Sidney Altman, who shared the Nobel Prize in Chemistry in 1989 for their finding that RNA could act as a catalyst. However, I am not sure about its significance with regard to the study of origin of life. RNA alone is not life. Just like I mentioned earlier, for me it may always remain as a mystery that how many different molecules could come together to form a primordial cell.

> *"RNA alone is not life. Just like I mentioned earlier, for me it may always remain as a mystery that how many different molecules could come together to form a primordial cell."*
>
> — Werner Arber

TDS: In many biology textbooks, the authors present very rosy and attractive theories about the generation of life from the assembly of chemicals in a cosmic time scale as if they are already happening. I am concerned that many innocent students may be misled with this approach.

WA: I am not sufficiently familiar with all the details but I think that we have to be practical. As a scientist I have learned not to believe too much in dogmatic theories given in textbooks.

TDS: It seems to me that in the study of life's origin, a multi-disciplinary approach incorporating many fields such as, biology, physics, theology and others, is quite important and necessary.

WA: Yes, I agree.

TDS: For some-time now, I have been thinking of how to incorporate the theological principles of life and its origin explained in the Vedanta into modern scientific study.

Vedanta very clearly states that the individual living being called *ātman*[21] in the Sanskrit language, is an irreducible spiritual entity and not a product of molecular evolution. In other words, life comes along with cosmic creation.

WA: I see your point. But it is not so easy to accord this with scientific knowledge.

TDS: The Austrian physicist Erwin Schrödinger wrote a classic monograph - *What is life?* in 1944. There he referred to the *Upaniṣads*, the philosophical aspects of Vedanta. He tried to introduce some aspects of the *Upaniṣads*. As a well-known quantum physicist, his approach in trying to understand life was quite open. He did not put up any cultural or religious barriers. In fact, he very much appreciated the Indian spiritual concept of the understanding of life.

Schrödinger's Monograph (1944)

WA: Yes, actually it is a very important book.

TDS: A few years ago, I attended the Nobel Forum held at the University of California, Berkeley. All the Nobel Laureates there unanimously declared that the present century would be the century of Biology.

WA: I share this opinion. We now have a number of novel research strategies to explore various aspects of life, but we still have many, many questions! And by far not all expectations can be fulfilled. For example, some people claim that genetic engineering will allow them to make novel types of living beings. To my mind, this view is highly exaggerated. Not a single gene has yet been invented by scientists. All those genes that one uses today are found somewhere in nature.

TDS: Yes, in bioengineering and biotechnology, scientists are hoping that a lot of new things will happen.

WA: In a discussion some years ago a prominent scientist expressed his hopes that it will soon be feasible to construct a fully novel living being. To be more precise I asked him to respect the two following conditions: Firstly, the novel construct should be at least a single cellular organism like a bacterial cell, and, secondly, no already known DNA sequences or entire genes should be used. In our discussion this scientist felt that these conditions could be respected and that the expected success might still be possible. I personally cannot agree with this claim.

> *"During this 21st century we may see the development of many extraordinary aspects of life – including the spiritual aspect, I hope. We may have the opportunity to take a good look into theism and atheism through the study of life sciences in the 21st century."*
>
> — T. D. Singh

TDS: Bioengineering and biotechnology have also raised a lot of bioethical questions. During this 21st century we may see the development of many extraordinary aspects of life – including the spiritual aspect, I hope. We may have the opportunity to take a good look into theism and atheism through the study of life sciences in the 21st century. We have to go on with our dialogue on life with many different thinkers in science, philosophy and theology. In one way or the other, it will be a very exciting century in the study of the life sciences.

WA: Yes, I hope so.

TDS: Recently in an Indian newspaper, there was a long article about "Einstein's Cosmic Religion". In this connection Einstein's dialogue with Tagore was also mentioned. Einstein's philosophical statement on science and religion – "Science without religion is lame, religion without science is blind" has been quoted quite often in many academic corners of the world. His statement, "I assert that the cosmic religious experience is the strongest and the noblest driving force behind scientific research" is extremely interesting.

WA: Some of his ideas are very outspoken.

TDS: As a scientist do you sometimes think about the concept of God and the divine inspiration in scientific work as well as the philosophy of life?

WA: Yes. Sometimes I think about God. However, I came to no final valid conclusion yet. It is difficult. For many people around here, God is only for humans. It may be different in India. I suppose you think differently.

TDS: According to the ancient Vedic science of India, God is the original seed of all living beings, *bijam mām' sarva-bhūtānām* (*Bhagavadgītā* 7.10). He is the original Supreme Personality, *ādi-puruṣa* and He is the benefactor and well-wisher not only for human beings but also for all other living beings.

WA: For me, as a biologist, that view may sound reasonable. In one of my earlier articles I wrote that humans should be less anthropocentric in their thoughts. Many people around here believe that only humans have souls. Perhaps your philosophy and religion are wider and more open than ours.

TDS: Thank you very much Prof. Arber, for your illuminating insights. It is extremely inspiring talking to you.

WA: I thank you for your visit and I hope to see you again.

———

Notes and References

1 Vedantic Tradition: Broadly, it is the tradition that is based upon the scientific, philosophical and theological teachings of the vedas.

2 Chemical evolutionists: Scientists who are investigating the origin of life with two key assumptions. The first assumption is that the life on earth arises through the reactions of four main chemical elements (hydrogen, oxygen, carbon and nitrogen). The second assumption is that matter will organize itself to form the biomonomers and that these monomers will polymerize to form the polysaccharides, nucleic acids and proteins of the cell. The scenario of chemical evolution is that these polymers will self-organize and, eventually some protocell is assumed to appear.

3 Molecular Evolutionists: Same as 'chemical evolutionists'.

4 Enzymes: A class of proteins serving as catalysts in biochemical reactions. Each enzyme is specific to a particular reaction or group of similar reactions.

5 Vedanta: See page 51.

6 Law of *Karma* states that every living entity has a predestined happiness and distress in his/her present body according to the actions performed by the living entity in his/her previous and present life.

7 Nucleotide: An organic compound consisting of a nitrogen-containing purine or pyridimine base linked to a sugar (ribose or deoxyribose) and a phosphate group. DNA and RNA are made up of long chains of nucleotides.

8 Substrate: The substance upon which an enzyme acts in biochemical reactions.

9 Horizontal Gene Transfer: The transfer of genetic information from one genome to other, specifically between two species.

10 Genome: The complete complement of an organism's genes; an organism's genetic material. All the genes contained in a single set of chromosome, i.e. in a haploid nucleus. Each parent, through its reproductive cells, contributes its genome to its offspring.

11 *Parā vidyā*: Knowledge about the spiritual world, spiritual life, spiritual identity and the spirit soul is called *parā vidyā*. By *parā vidyā* one can understand the *akṣara-Brahman* or the Absolute Truth.

12 *Aparā vidyā*: Material knowledge.

13 *Upaniṣads*: philosophical portions of the Vedas. There are 108 *Upaniṣads*.

14 Vedas: The word veda literally means "knowledge", and thus in

a wider sense it refers to the whole body of Indian Sanskrit religious literature that is in harmony with the philosophical conclusions found in the four original Vedic scriptures, *Saṁhitās* (*Ṛg*, *Sāma*, *Atharva* and *Yajur*), 108 *Upaniṣads*, *Mahābhārata*, *Vedānta-sūtra*, etc.

15 This philosophy was propagated by the great saint of medieval Bengal Śrī Caitanya Mahāprabhu. Everything is simultaneously one with and different from everything else. The cosmic manifestation created by the Supreme Lord by His material energy is also simultaneously different and nondifferent from Him. The material energy is non-different from the Supreme Lord, but at the same time, because that energy is acting in a different way, it is different from Him. Similarly, the individual living entity is one with and different from the Supreme Lord. This 'simultaneously oneness and difference' philosophy is the perfect theistic conclusion of the *Bhāgavata* school.

16 Pathogenicity: Ability of an organism to cause disease.

17 Polymer Chain Reaction(PCR): A technique used to replicate a fragment of DNA so as to produce many copies of a particular DNA sequence. PCR is commonly employed as an alternative to gene cloning as a means for amplifying genetic material for gene sequencing, and is also used to measure gene expression. The technique has also proved invaluable in forensic science, enabling amplification of minute traces of genetic material for DNA fingerprinting. The two strands of DNA are separated by heating and short sequences of a single DNA strands (primers) are added, together with a supply of free nucleotides and DNA polymerase obtained from a bacterium that can withstand extreme heat. In a series of heating and cooling cyles, the DNA sequence doubles with each cycle and is thus rapidly amplified.

18 Primers: Short sequences of a single DNA strand.

19 Thomas. R. Cech and Sidney Altman were awarded the Nobel prize in chemistry in 1989.

20 RNA World: In the late 1960s, several biologists, including Crick, proposed that the ancestor molecule was neither DNA nor a protein, but RNA, the versatile messenger molecule. RNA, they suggested, might have catalyzed reactions necessary for replication as well as providing the genetic information necessary to replicate itself. In the 1980s, Thomas Cech and Sidney Altman independently discovered a kind of RNA that catalyzes a reaction — it "splices" out the parts of a gene that have no function in protein coding. The discovery of this RNA enzyme, or ribozyme, revived interest in the earlier

conjecture that RNA might have been the original genetic material. In an article in *Nature* in 1986 , Walter Gilbert outlined an evolutionary scenario called the "RNA World," in which RNA molecules catalyze their own replications, then evolve to be able to undertake "a range of enzymatic activities, including the synthesis of proteins, and are finally superseded as the primary storehouse of genetic information by the much less versatile, but much more stable DNA, which is created by a process of reverse transcription. Since Cech and Altman were awarded the Nobel prize in 1989 for their discovery of enzyme catalysis, research into the RNA World theory has exploded. No RNA molecule long enough to encode an entire gene has yet been developed. Although it seems to be a widely accepted account of the origin of self-replication, RNA World has also its detractors. Leslie Orgel, one of the scientists who first proposed it in the 1960s, still thinks that RNA played an important role in the development of early life, but he concedes that researchers who have attempted to illustrate the possibility of spontaneous generation of the chemical elements of RNA itself have had only modest success. Of particular concern is the fact that ribose, the sugar that is part of the backbone of the RNA molecule, is difficult to create from hypothetical early earth conditions except in very small quantities. Another objection to the RNA World theory is that even if RNA could have formed spontaneously, extreme conditions on the primitive earth might have led to rapid chemical degradation of it.

21 Ātmān: the self or soul.

BIOGRAPHICAL INFORMATION OF
CONTRIBUTORS

 T. D. Singh (1937-2006): A scientist and spiritualist known for his pioneering efforts to interface between science and religion for a deeper understanding of life and the universe, he received his Ph.D. in Physical Organic Chemistry from the University of California, Irvine in 1974. He has contributed many papers in the *Journal of American Chemical Society* and the *Journal of Organic Chemistry* in the field of fast proton transfer kinetics in model biological systems using stopped-flow technique and NMR spectroscopy. He also worked on gas phase reaction mechanisms using Ion Cyclotron Resonance (ICR) spectroscopy. He underwent Vaishnava Vedanta Studies (1970-77) under His Divine Grace Śrīla Prabhupāda and was appointed as Director of the Bhaktivedanta Institute (1974-) which is a center to promote studies about the relationaship between science and vedanta. He has organized three International conferences on science and religion — First and Second World Congress for the Synthesis of Science and Religion (1986 & 1997) and First International Conference on the Study of Consciousness within Science (1990) where a galaxy of prominent scientists and religious leaders including several Nobel Laureates participated. He has authored and edited several books including *What is Matter and What is Life?* (1977), *Theobiology* (1979), *Vedanta and Science Series: Life and Origin of the Universe* (2004), *Life and Spiritual Evolution* (2005), *Essays on Science and Religion* (2005), *(Ed.) Synthesis of Science and Religion: Critical Essays and Dialogues* (1987), *Thoughts on Synthesis of Science and Religion* (2001), *Seven Nobel Laureates on Science and Spirituality* (2004), *Science, Spirituality and the Nature of Reality* (2005). He was also the Founder Editor-in-Chief of *Savijnanam – Scientific Exploration for a Spiritual Paradigm*, the Journal of the Bhaktivedanta Institute.

 The Dalai Lama (1935-): The XIVth Dalai Lama, Tenzin Gyatso was born in 1935 in a small village called Takster in northeastern Tibet. He began his education at the age of six and completed the Geshe Lharampa Degree (Doctorate of Buddhist Philosophy) when he was 25. At 24, he took the preliminary examination at each of the three monastic universities: Drepung, Sera and Ganden. In 1950, he was called upon to assume full political power as Head of State and Government when Tibet was threatened by the might of China. In 1959 he was forced into exile in India after the Chinese military occupation of Tibet and since 1960 he has resided and set up a government-in-exile in Dharmsala, India. In 1989 he was awarded the Nobel Prize in Peace. He has written a number of books on Tibetan Buddhism and an autobiography *Freedom in Exile – The Autobiography of the Dalai Lama* (1990).

George Wald (1906-1997): Born in New York City on November 18th, 1906. He received Bachelor of Science degree (1927) from Washington Square College, New York University; and Ph.D. (1932) from Columbia University. On receiving the Ph. D. he was awarded a National Research Council Fellowship in Biology (1932-1934). This was begun in the laboratory of Otto Warburg in Berlin-Dahlem and it was there that Dr.Wald first identified vitamin A in the retina. He then served at Harvard as Instructor and Tutor in Biology (1935-1939); Faculty Instructor (1939-1944); Associate Professor (1944-1948); and Professor of Biology (since 1948). His research on vision included the comparison of retinas in different organisms and the discovery of retinene, a fundamental chemical agent in vision. He published much of his research in scientific journals. His long career as a vision scientist and physiologist culminated in his discovery of how Vitamin A works in the retina, leading to the understanding of the chemical basis of vision. He received (with Haldan K. Hartline of the United States and Ragnar Granit of Sweden) the Nobel Prize for Physiology and Medicine in 1967 for his work on the chemistry of vision. He became professor emeritus at Harvard in 1977.

Charles H. Townes (1915-): Born on July 28, 1915 in Greenville, South Carolina, U.S.; Received B.A. and B. S. (1935), Furman University; M.A. (1937), Duke University; Ph.D. (1939), California Institute of Technology; Member (1939-1947) of the Technical staff, Bell Telephone Laboratories, Inc.; Associate Professor (1948-1950) and Professor (1950-1961) at Columbia University; Served (1959-1961) as Vice President and Director of Research at the Institute for Defense Analyses, Washington, D.C.; Provost and Professor (1961-1966) of Physics at Massachusetts Institute of Technology, Cambridge; University Professor of Physics (1967-1986) and Emeritus Professor (1986-1994), University of California, Berkeley; Professor (1994 onwards), Graduate School, University of California, Berkeley;

Author of several books including *Making Waves* and *Unturned Stones*; Received Nobel Prize for Physics in 1964 for his role in the invention of the maser and the laser and numerous other awards and honors.

 Betty Williams (1943-): Born in Belfast (Ireland) in 1943. Northern Irish Peace Activist, received Nobel Peace Prize in 1976. Moved to the United States in 1981 and traveled extensively throughout the country; Received numerous honors other than the Nobel Peace Prize, such as an Honorary Doctor of Law degree from the Yale University, the Schweitzer Medallion for Courage, the Martin Luther King Jr. Award, and the Eleanor Roosevelt Award; Appointed (1992) to the Texas Commission for Children and Youth by the Governor Ann Richards of Texas; Received (1995) the Rotary Club International "Paul Harris Fellowship"; Since 1997, President of the World Centers of Compassion for Children, Chair of The Institute for Asian Democracy in Washington, D.C., and Visiting Distinguished Scholar at Florida Atlantic University in Boca Raton, Florida.

 B. D. Josephson (1940-): Born on Jan. 4, 1940 in Cardiff, Wales, U.K. He received his bachelor's (1960) and master's and Ph.D. degrees (1964) from Trinity College, Cambridge. He was elected a fellow of Trinity College in 1962. He went to the United States to be a research professor at the University of Illinois in 1965-66 and in 1967 returned to Cambridge as assistant director of research, University of Cambridge. He was appointed as professor of physics in 1974. He showed theoretically that tunneling between two superconductors could have very special characteristics, *e.g.*, flow across an insulating layer without the application of a voltage; if a voltage is applied, the current stops flowing and oscillates at high frequency. This was the Josephson effect. His discovery of the Josephson effect won him Nobel Prize for Physics in 1973. Other than many papers published by him, he also published in 1980, along with V. S. Ramachandran, an edited transcript of a 1978 international symposium on consciousness at Oxford under the title *Consciousness and the Physical World.*

 Richard R. Ernst (1933-): Born in 1933 in Winterthur, Switzerland; Diploma in Chemistry in 1957, Ph. D. in Technical Sciences in 1962 from the Swiss Federal Institute of Technology in Zurich (ETH-Z); Received Honorary Doctorate degrees of ETH Lausanne,

Technische Universitat Munich, Universitat Zurich, University Antwerpen, Babes-Bolyai University, Cluj-Napoca, and University Montpellier; Professor of Physical Chemistry since 1976, Director of the Physical Chemistry Laboratory of the ETH Zurich, retired in 1998; was awarded the Nobel Prize in Chemistry in 1991 for his contributions to Fourier Transform NMR and for subsequent contributions to Two-Dimensional NMR Spectroscopy; also received the Marcel Benoist Prize in 1986, the Wolf Prize for Chemistry in1991 and the Horwitz Prize in 1991.

 Werner Arber (1929-): A well-known microbiologist, he was awarded the Nobel Prize in Physiology and Medicine in 1978 for the discovery of the restriction enzymes and their application to problems of molecular genetics. The discovery of restriction enzymes provided new tools for the detailed chemical analysis of the mechanism of gene action and opened new paths to genetic engineering and gene therapy. From 1949 to 1953, he studied towards the diploma in Natural Sciences at the Swiss Polytechnical School in Zurich. He earned his Ph. D. in 1958 and took faculty position in 1960 at the University of Geneva. After serving as the faculty at Geneva from 1960 to 1970, he became professor of molecular biology at Biozentrum Research Institute, University of Basel, Switzerland in 1971. He received several awards and honors including the Platamour-Prevost prize of the University of Geneva (1962) and a grant from Swiss National Science Foundation (1965-1970). He has also served as the President (1996-1999) of the International Council for Science (ICS), a worldwide non-governmental organization of scientists. He has contributed several papers in the *Journal of Molecular Evolution, Molecular Genetics and Genomics,* etc., and has edited the book *Genetic Manipulation: Impact on Man and Society* (1984).

THE BHAKTIVEDANTA INSTITUTE

The Bhaktivedanta Institute was founded by His Divine Grace A. C. Bhaktivedānta Swami Prabhupāda in Vrindavan in August 1974. Śrīla Prabhupāda was one of the greatest exponents of Vedic culture in the 20th Century. He strongly felt that modern civilization is completely misdirected by scientific materialism and there is an urgent need to introduce the spiritual knowledge and wisdom of the *Bhagavad-gītā* and the *Śrīmad-Bhāgavatam*, the cream of all the Vedic literatures, to the scientists, philosophers, scholars and students of the world. He noticed that all the prestigious academic institutions and universities of the world were teaching many different subjects but they had left out the most important branch of knowledge – the science of the soul. He envisioned that this spiritual knowledge of life would help restore an ethical culture for modern society. Thus, there would be hope for bringing lasting happiness and world peace. He felt that introducing this spiritual culture should be the contribution of India for the welfare of humanity. Śrīla Prabhupāda appointed his disciple Dr. T. D. Singh (Bhaktisvarūpa Dāmodara Swami) as the director of the Insitute from its very inception and left several instructions to him to carry forward his vision.

The Bhaktivedanta Institute is a center for Advanced Studies in Science and Vedānta and focuses on a consciousness-based paradigm. This spiritual paradigm has a unique potential to resolve the mind-body problem, the question of evolution and life's origin and many other philosophical and ethical concerns. Thus this paradigm will have profound significance for science, religion, and their synthesis. One of the primary objectives of the Bhaktivedanta Institute is to present this paradigm for the critical attention of serious scholars and thinkers throughout the world. As such, the institute supports a closer examination of existing scientific paradigms in cosmology, evolution, physics, biology, and other sciences. The institute also promotes scientific, philosophical and religious dialogues among scientists, scholars and theologians of the world covering various common conceptual grounds of science and religion for the purpose of creating a better and harmonious understanding among all people. In order to achieve these goals the institute organizes international conferences regularly and publishes books and journals. Interested persons may contact the secretary of the Institute at:

The Bhaktivedanta Institute,
RC-8, Raghunathpur,
Manasi Manjil Building, Fourth Floor
VIP Road, Kolkata 700 059, India
Tel: +91-33-2500-9018; Fax: +91-33-2500-6091
email: bi@binstitute.org
website: www.binstitute.org

SAVIJÑĀNAM
Scientific Exploration for a Spiritual Paradigm
Journal of the Bhaktivedanta Institute

ISSN: 0972-6586

Savijñānam — Scientific Exploration for a Spiritual Paradigm is the annual multidisciplinary Journal of the Bhaktivedanta Institute. One of the main aims of the journal is to explore the link between science and spirituality. The journal serves as an open forum where thoughts relating to spiritual paradigms can be scientifically presented. The first issue of the journal (November 2002) includes dialogues with **Prof. Werner Arber**, a *well-known microbiologist at the University of Basel, Switzerland, who received Nobel prize in medicine and physiology* and another dialogue with **Prof. Karl H. Pribram,** a *neuropsychologist from Georgetown University, Washington D.C.* The second issue of the journal (December 2003) includes a dialogue on 'Science and Spiritual Exploration' with **Prof. Charles H. Townes**, *a Nobel Laureate in Physics from the University of California, Berkeley, USA* and many other articles. To subscribe this journal (subscription form attached on next page), please write to:

Prof. Werner Arber
Nobel Laureate in Medicine and Physiology, University of Basel, Switzerland

Prof. Charles Townes
Nobel Laureate in Physics, University of California, Berkeley, USA

Prof. Karl H. Pribram
Neuropsychologist, Georgetown University, Washington D.C.

Prof. Amit Goswami
Quantum Physicist University of Oregon, Eugene, USA

Founder
Editor-in-Chief

Dr. T. D. Singh
Physical Organic Chemist; Founder Director, Bhaktivedanta Institute

The Bhaktivedanta Institute

RC-8, Raghunathpur,
Manasi Manjil Building, Fourth Floor
VIP Road, Kolkata 700 059, India
Tel: +91-33-2500-9018; Fax: +91-33-2500-6091
email: bi@binstitute.org
website: www.binstitute.org

Subscription Form

SAVIJÑĀNAM

Scientific Exploration for a Spiritual Paradigm
Journal of the Bhaktivedanta Institute
(ISSN: 0972 - 6586)

Subscription Rates (one issue per year): India/Rest of the World

	❏ 4 issues		❏ 6 issues		❏ 8 issues	
	Rs.	US$	Rs.	US$	Rs.	US$
❏ Students:*	225	34	325	50	425	65
❏ Individuals:	250	36	360	53	470	69
❏ Institutions:	450	40	650	59	825	77

Please provide a xerox copy of valid student ID.
Note: *Please add bank clearing charges for outstation cheques:*
India: Rs. 50; Outside India: US$ 5 for amount less than US$ 50; US$ 10 for amount more than US$ 50

Vol. 1   Vol. 2   Vol. 3-4   Vol. 5-6

You can also subscribe online at www.binstitute.org/journal/subscribe.php

This form is to be mailed by the subscriber to the Bhaktivedanta Institute's address.

www.binstitute.org
bi@binstitute.org

Please fill in block letters:

Name: ....

Address: ....

City: .... State: .... Country: .... ZIP: ....

Tel: .... Fax: .... Email: ....

❏ Demand Draft ❏ Cheque enclosed (Payable to 'Bhaktivedanta Institute')

❏ Cash for Rs/US$ .... No.: .... Dated: .... Bank: ....

Please start my subscription from vol. no.: _____

❏ Yes, I am also interested to receive the previous issues of **SAVIJÑĀNAM**-*Scientific Exploration for a Spiritual Paradigm.* Kindly send me the information about the previous issues.

Please mail the duly filled form to:
Bhaktivedanta Institute
RC/8, Raghunathpur, Manasi Manjil Building,
Fourth Floor, VIP Road, Kolkata 700 059, India
Tel: +91-33-2500-9018, Fax: +91-33-2500-6091

Representative's Details (if applicable):
Name: ....
Mobile: ....
Email: ....
Amount received: .... Rep. Sign: ....

THOUGHTS ON SYNTHESIS
OF SCIENCE AND RELIGION

Edited by T. D. Singh & S. Bandyopadhyay
pp.735, Hardbound; 16 Color plates.
ISBN: 81-901369-0-9

This major publication by the Bhaktivedanta Institute contains learned articles on the synthesis of science and religion from **42 eminent scholars, religious leaders and scientists of the world including five Nobel Laureates**. The volume was formally released as a part of annual **Indian Science Congress** and is highly appreciated by the **President of India Dr. A. P. J. Abdul Kalam**. Containing 7 main sections, the volume reflects some possible grounds for the synthesis of science and religion and covers a wide variety of subject matters including faith, ethics, culture, consciousness, biology, quantum mechanics, Ecology/Environment, Biomedical Ethics for the 21st Century, and World Peace. It further explores the exciting and evocative work emerging in the fields of neuroscience, artificial intelligence, cognitive science, psychology, philosophy and a vast body of spiritual and religious experiences.

Buy online at:
www.binstitute.org

ORDER FORM

Thoughts on Synthesis of Science and Religion

Price: India: Rs 1150.00; Rest of the World: US$ 25.00
Shipping and Handling Charges: Rs 45.00 (India) / US$ 5.00 (Outside India)

Name: ....

Address: ....

....

Tel: .... Fax: .... email: ....

Demand Draft/Cheque enclosed (Payble to 'Bhaktivedanta Institute')
of Rs/US$ .... No.: .... Dated:...................